# From Contemplation to Action

# From Contemplation to Action

## The Spiritual Process of Divine Discernment Using Elijah and Elisha as Models

MARK G. BOYER

WIPF & STOCK · Eugene, Oregon

FROM CONTEMPLATION TO ACTION
The Spiritual Process of Divine Discernment Using Elijah and Elisha as Models

Copyright © 2018 Mark G. Boyer. All rights reserved. Except for brief quotations in critical publications or reviews, no part of this book may be reproduced in any manner without prior written permission from the publisher. Write: Permissions, Wipf and Stock Publishers, 199 W. 8th Ave., Suite 3, Eugene, OR 97401.

Wipf & Stock
An Imprint of Wipf and Stock Publishers
199 W. 8th Ave., Suite 3
Eugene, OR 97401

www.wipfandstock.com

PAPERBACK ISBN: 978-1-5326-5378-0
HARDCOVER ISBN: 978-1-5326-5379-7
EBOOK ISBN: 978-1-5326-5380-3

Manufactured in the U.S.A.  09/10/18

The Scripture quotations contained herein are from the New Revised Standard Version Bible, copyright © 1989 by the Division of Christian Education of the National Council of the Churches of Christ in the U.S.A., and are used by permission. All rights reserved.

Dedicated to my godson,
Zachary Douglas Kinler,
and his bride,
Elsa Anne Kavajecz,
September 16, 2018,
their greatest adventure ever.

"… A mystic is simply one who has moved from mere belief or belonging to actual inner experience of God.... Without a contemplative mind, we are offering the world no broad seeing, no real alternative consciousness, no new kind of humanity. Unless people have had some mystical, inner spiritual experience,... [they] don't have the power to follow any of Jesus' major teachings about forgiveness, love of enemies, nonviolence, humble use of power, and so on, except in and through radical union with God."

—Richard Rohr

"… [T]he choreography for prayer includes three steps: devotional active praying, a more passive prophetic receiving from God that requires a response on the part of the pray-er, and a degree of mystical transcendence."

"… [B]reathing is to physical life what praying is to spiritual life.... [V]arying prayer activities promote ongoing spiritual transformation.... Prayer is about having a romance with the Divine."

—*The Heart of Religion*

# Contents

*Abbreviations* • ix
*Notes on the Bible* • xiii
*Characters* • xv
*Introduction* • xix

## 1 Elijah • 1

Elijah Appears • 2
Water and Food • 3
Zarephath • 5
Revived Son • 6
The Plan: Part 1 • 8
The Plan: Part 2 • 10
Terms of the Contest • 11
No Answer • 12
Preparing a Theophany • 13
End of Drought • 15
Fleeing for Life • 16
Under the Broom Tree • 17
Sheer Silence • 19
Elisha Appears • 22
Naboth's Vineyard: Part 1 • 23
Naboth's Vineyard: Part 2 • 25
Ahaziah's Death • 27
Preparation to Leave • 30
Elijah's Disappearance • 32

| | |
|---|---:|
| Elijah's Power | 36 |
| Elijah Summary | 39 |

## 2  Elisha — 41

| | |
|---|---:|
| Purified Spring | 42 |
| Bears | 44 |
| Wadi Pools | 45 |
| Oil | 48 |
| Shunammite Couple | 49 |
| Resuscitation | 51 |
| Purified Stew | 53 |
| Loaves | 55 |
| Naaman: Part 1 | 57 |
| Naaman: Part 2 | 58 |
| Naaman: Part 3 | 60 |
| Naaman: Part 4 | 62 |
| Naaman: Part 5 | 64 |
| Floating Ax Head | 66 |
| All-Knowing | 68 |
| Samaria under Siege: Part 1 | 70 |
| Samaria under Siege: Part 2 | 72 |
| Shunammite Woman again | 76 |
| Hazael Becomes King | 77 |
| Jehu Becomes King | 79 |
| Arrows | 82 |
| Elisha's Death | 83 |
| Elisha Summary | 86 |
| *Recent Books by Mark G. Boyer* | 89 |

# Abbreviations

| | |
|---|---|
| BCE | Before the Common Era (same as BC = Before Christ) |
| CE | Common Era (same as AD = *Anno Domini*, in the year of the Lord) |

## **CB (NT)**    **Christian Bible (New Testament)**

| | |
|---|---|
| Acts | Acts of the Apostles |
| Heb | Letter to the Hebrews |
| Jas | Letter of James |
| John | John's Gospel |
| Luke | Luke's Gospel |
| Mark | Mark's Gospel |
| Matt | Matthew's Gospel |
| Rom | Letter of Paul to the Romans |

## **HB (OT)**    **Hebrew Bible (Old Testament)**

| | |
|---|---|
| 1 Chr | First Book of Chronicles |
| 2 Chr | Second Book of Chronicles |
| Deut | Deuteronomy |
| Eccl | Ecclesiastes |

## Abbreviations

| | |
|---|---|
| Exod | Exodus |
| Ezek | Ezekiel |
| Gen | Genesis |
| Hab | Habbakkuk |
| Hos | Hosea |
| Isa | Isaiah |
| Jer | Jeremiah |
| Job | Job |
| Josh | Joshua |
| 1 Kgs | First Book of Kings |
| 2 Kgs | Second Book of Kings |
| Lam | Lamentations |
| Lev | Leviticus |
| Mal | Malachi |
| Nah | Nahum |
| Num | Numbers |
| Ps | Psalm |
| 1 Sam | First Book of Samuel |
| 2 Sam | Second Book of Samuel |
| Zech | Zechariah |

ABBREVIATIONS

**OT (A)**     **Old Testament (Apocrypha)**

2 Esd     Second Book of Esdras

1 Macc     First Book of Maccabees

Sir     Sirach (Ecclesiasticus)

Wis     Wisdom (of Solomon)

# Notes on the Bible

THE BIBLE IS DIVIDED into two parts: The Hebrew Bible (Old Testament) and the Christian Bible (New Testament). The Hebrew Bible consists of thirty-nine named books accepted by Jews and Protestants as Holy Scripture. The Old Testament also contains those thirty-nine books plus seven to fifteen more named books or parts of books called the Apocrypha or the Deuterocanonical Books; the Old Testament is accepted by Catholics and several other Christian denominations as Holy Scripture. The Christian Bible, consisting of twenty-seven named books, is also called the New Testament; it is accepted by Christians as Holy Scripture. Thus, in this work:

—Hebrew Bible (Old Testament), abbreviated HB (OT), indicates that a book is found both in the Hebrew Bible and the Old Testament;

—Old Testament (Apocrypha), abbreviated OT (A), indicates that a book is found only in the Old Testament Apocrypha and not in the Hebrew Bible;

—and Christian Bible (New Testament), abbreviated CB (NT), indicates that a book is found only in the Christian Bible or New Testament.

In noting biblical texts, the first number refers to the chapter in the book, and the second number refers to the verse within the chapter. Thus, HB (OT) Isa 7:11 means that the quotation comes from Isaiah, chapter 7, verse 11. OT (A) Sirach 39:30 means that the quotation comes from Sirach, chapter 39, verse 30. CB (NT) Mark 6:2 means that the quotation comes from Mark's Gospel, chapter 6, verse 2. When more than one sentence appears in a verse, the letters a, b, c, etc. indicate the sentence being referenced in the verse. Thus, HB (OT) 2 Kgs 1:6a means that the quotation comes from the Second Book of Kings, chapter 1, verse 6, sentence 1.

In the HB (OT) and the OT (A), the reader often sees LORD (note all capital letters). Because God's name (Yahweh or YHWH, referred to as the Tetragrammaton) is not to be pronounced, the name Adonai (meaning *Lord*) is substituted for Yahweh when a biblical text is read. When a biblical text is translated and printed, LORD (cf. Gen 2:4) is used to alert the reader to what the text actually states: Yahweh. Furthermore, when the biblical author writes Lord Yahweh, printers present Lord GOD (note all capital letters for GOD; cf. Gen 15:2) to avoid the printed ambiguity of LORD LORD. When the reference is to Jesus, the word printed is Lord (note capital L and lower case letters; cf. Luke 11:1). When writing about a lord (note all lower case letters (cf. Matt 18:25) with servants, no capital L is used.

# Characters

IN THE ELIJAH-ELISHA CYCLE of biblical stories, a number of characters appear. The following alphabetical list is presented as an aid to the reader.

| | |
|---|---|
| Abraham | founder of the Hebrews |
| Ahab | son of Omri, King of Israel (874–853 BCE) |
| Ahaziah | son of Ahab, King of Israel (853–852 BCE) |
| Ahaziah | succeeds Jehoram, King of Judah (843 BCE), killed by Jehu |
| Asherah | Canaanite goddess, consort of Baal |

# Characters

| | |
|---|---|
| Athaliah | daughter of Ahab, married to King Jehoram of Judah, queen mother (843–838 BCE) |
| Baal | fertility god worshiped by Ahab and Jezebel |
| Ben-hadad | King of Damascus (880–842 BCE) |
| company of prophets | group of prophets who live together, some of whom are married |
| Elisha | son of Shaphat, successor to Elijah, eighth-century BCE prophet in Israel |
| Elijah | eighth-century BCE prophet in Israel |
| Gehazi | servant of Elisha |
| Hazael | succeeds Ben-hadad, King of Damascus (842–806 BCE) |
| Isaac | son of Abraham, father of Jacob |
| Israel | other name for Jacob, son of Isaac; name of the Northern Kingdom |
| Jehoash | called Joash, succeeds Jehoahaz, King of Israel (801–786 BCE) |
| Jehoahaz | succeeds Jehu, King of Israel (816–801 BCE) |
| Jehoram | called Joram, son of Ahab, King of Israel (852–843 BCE) |
| Jehoram | succeeds Jehoshaphat, King of Judah (849–843 BCE), married to Athaliah |
| Jehoshaphat | King of Judah (870–849 BCE) |

## Characters

| | |
|---|---|
| Jehu | son of Nimshi, succeeds Jehoram (Joram), King of Israel (843–816) |
| Jezebel | daughter of Ethbaal of Sidon, wife-queen of Ahab, fosters worship of Baal |
| Joash | kept alive by Jehosheba, succeeds Athaliah, King of Judah (838–800 BCE) |
| LORD | replaces YHWH (Yahweh) in biblical translations |
| Moses | leader of the Hebrews (Israelites, Jews) out of Egyptian slavery |
| Naaman | leprous, Aramean army commander healed by Elisha |
| Naboth | owner of a vineyard in Jezreel; murdered by the plot of Jezebel and Ahab |
| Obadiah | chief steward of Ahab |

## Royal Chronology during the Time of Elijah and Elisha

*Kings of Israel*

Ahab (874–853 BCE)

Ahaziah (853–852 BCE)

Jehoram (Joram) (852–843 BCE)

Jehu (843–816 BCE)

Jehoahaz (816–801 BCE)

Jehoash (Joash) (801–786 BCE)

# Characters

*Kings of Judah*

Jehoshaphat (870–849 BCE)

Jehoram (849–843 BCE)

Ahaziah (843 BCE)

Athaliah, queen mother (843–838 BCE)

Joash (838–800 BCE)

*Kings of Damascus (Aram)*

Ben-hadad II (880–842 BCE)

Hazael (842–806 BCE)

Ben-hadad III (806–?)

# Introduction

## CONTEMPLATION AND ACTION

CONTEMPLATION IS A SPIRITUAL process involving long, thoughtful, steady, serious, and attentive consideration or observation. It is deep spiritual thought or meditation in order to achieve closer unity with God and to discover and understand God's will for the contemplative. Once a person understands or grasps inspired insights into God's spiritual work, then he or she has discerned God's will. However, the activity draws the person into even deeper contemplation to discover further refinement, deeper perception, and greater connectivity that flows outward into more activity.

Contemplation is best done in solitude. Sitting, standing, walking, or kneeling alone in silence fosters stillness within a person that raises his or her awareness to the presence of God within. Simplicity free from the distractions of telephones, computers, radios, TVs, and other people enables solitude and, consequently, transformation from dullness to awareness of the divine presence. Only in solitary silence can a person listen deeply to his or her life and know the change that leads to transformation of self.

# Introduction

The basic meaning of conversion is a strong commitment to the process of transformation so that one is aware that God lives in him or her more than he or she lives in himself or herself. One must consent to transformation, which takes place through the dispossessing of all one lays claim to, such as body, mind, and spirit. When one has nothing, then one has all!

It is not a matter of contemplation or action, but one of contemplation and action, action and contemplation. They are in dialogue with each other. Contemplation gives rise to activity, and activity, in turn, gives rise to more contemplation. For way too long, the focus of spirituality has been on either one or the other without melding them into a simple process. This book is an attempt to escape the dualism of contemplation and activity in (the spiritual) life and present them as one process of spiritual reciprocity. As will be explained below, the very process presented for each exercise moves from contemplation of Scripture to activity that flows from the contemplation and leads the reader back to deeper contemplation. While traveling the road from contemplation to action and back to contemplation, the individual discovers ongoing spiritual transformation. In other words, listening deeply in silent solitude brings one in contact with his or her spirit, which is a manifestation of Spirit. The result of the process is spirituality.

People search diligently for God through all types of practices within and outside all world religions, and they give up in exhaustion when they haven't found the divine. Paradoxically, God cannot be found and can be found! God cannot be found by those who are less mighty than the all-powerful One. If a person can find God, then he or she is greater. God can be found by making contact with one's spirit; "[i]n him we live and move and have our being" (Acts 17:28a). Furthermore, God finds people; this is a fundamental biblical truth of spirituality that has been overwhelmed by individualism's quest to be in control of all of life. When people state that they cannot find God, it is because they don't know that he has already found them! Ear plugs, cell phones, blogs, tweets, etc. are distractions from solitary solitude and silence in which God finds people and their awareness is raised to recognize the event.

This paradoxical truth is hugged by those who make vows of silence—monks and nuns in monasteries and convents, hermits and anchorites in wilderness hermitages, and all men and women who choose to live as solitudinarians for all or part of their lives. They know how to be quiet within and without and hear God's voice in their own thoughts and words, in inspirited texts, and in nature surrounding them. Not only is such awareness known as inspiration, but it is spirituality through contemplation and action. Even ordinary people can be ministers of spirituality if one's clutter and noise is cleared away in order to receive it.

The result of contemplation is often called discernment, seeing clearly what is at first not very clear or obvious, understanding what is not immediately obvious, resulting in accuracy of spiritual perception. Divine discernment is contemplation in action; it results in insight, inspiration, and an awareness of inner truth upon which one must act. Contemplation, consciousness, or awareness reduces the distance between who people are and what they do. Only by knowing themselves can they set themselves free from themselves and discern carefully and spiritually what God is asking them to do. Often referred to as a spiritual awakening, a sudden awareness, a consciousness that one is connected to everything and everyone overwhelms a person. A person's whole being is taken over by God. He or she gets a transpersonal glimpse into the realm of existence—being—which shares Being and sets in motion the transformation process. In other words, one experiences intimacy with God.

Contemplation is initiation into the Godhead. Three Persons—Father, Son, Spirit—are absorbed in each other, gazing upon each other in absolute and total awareness. People connect and participate in that gazing through contemplation, that is, by being open to the fullness each Person wants to pour into their lives. This, of course, requires an emptying for each individual. One cannot be filled unless he or she is empty. Self-surrender, letting go in trust, or emptying is required so one can be filled and changed into a long-term process of growth that unveils deeper and deeper connectivity with everyone, everything, and God.

## PARADOX

CONTEMPLATION INVOLVES PARADOX. IN other words, it usually sounds absurd or contradictory. As noted above, God can be found, and God cannot be found. Only by spending time in solitary silence while going deeper and deeper in contemplation does truth begin to spill out of paradox. The spiritual life is built on bringing together what seems to be contradictory to or conflicting with conventional or common opinion. The contemplative sees that the duality is not the truth; unity is the truth. Often, one needs to let go of his or her idea of who God is and let God be whoever he is! When opposites are brought together, that is paradox. And that is why the biblical

Introduction

prophets Elijah and Elisha are used as models of contemplation that leads to action and back to contemplation; they were living examples of paradox, as will be seen in the entries below.

## ELIJAH AND ELISHA

BIBLICAL SCHOLARS THINK THAT the Elijah cycle of stories (1 Kgs 17:1–19:21, 21:1–29, 2 Kgs 1:1–2:12) is fashioned on the Elisha cycle of stories (2 Kgs 2:13–9:13, 13:14–21). While that may be true, this book follows the order of the events in the Elijah and Elisha cycles of stories as they appear in the First Book of Kings and the Second Book of Kings. Furthermore, while there are countless models of contemplation leading to action in the centuries before Jesus and after him, the ninth-century BCE prophets Elijah and Elisha are the examples used in this work. Both of them ministered in the Northern Kingdom of Israel; the kings there were focused on worship of Baal instead of worship of the LORD.

God sends Elijah from Gilead, a Tranjordanian region not part of Israel, to King Ahab and his two successor sons! The biblical model for Elijah is Moses. Thus, Elijah's ministry consists mostly of conflict with the royal house of Israel over syncretistic worship, just like Moses' conflict with pharaoh was about the most powerful God. Elijah, champion of the LORD, often opposes Jezebel, Ahab's wife and champion of Baal. Both Moses and Elijah begin their spiritual journey by fleeing eastward to escape the wrath of a king and find lodging with a family. Each reluctantly returns to his home to challenge a king and awaken faith in followers of the LORD. Each makes a journey to Mount Horeb (Sinai) where he experiences a theophany after building an altar. Each receives a mission from the LORD, whose presence is manifested on the mountain with natural phenomena. Furthermore, each is fed by the LORD, and each mysteriously disappears after death.

Elisha, Elijah's successor from Abel-meholah, is designated by the LORD, and he is transformed into Elijah's heir with the receipt of Elijah's power as the latter ascends into heaven in a whirlwind while riding in a fiery chariot pulled by fiery horses. The biblical model for Elisha is Elijah. Elisha makes a journey with Elijah, crossing the Jordan River, and receiving Elijah's spirit, thus making him a new Elijah. Like Elijah, Elisha stays with a family and raises the son from the dead. He ministers to a widow, like Elijah, and, while working more wonders than his predecessor, Elisha, leader of a company of prophets, is often depicted as spending time alone.

INTRODUCTION

Both prophets are called a man of God. They are spiritual power brokers. Both are seers, messengers, and heralds of the LORD. They appear in activity when they are needed, and they disappear into solitude and silence when they are not. Their power persists even after their death; Elijah's is found in his mantle, and Elisha's is found in his bones. Furthermore, the influence of these prophets can be found in the Christian Bible (New Testament). Their words and deeds undeniably underlie many of the narratives of the words and deeds of Jesus. In other words, the stories about Elijah and Elisha serve as types or models which could readily be used and understood by ancient oral story tellers and captured in print by later writers of records about Jesus which have come to be known as gospels. Thus, at appropriate places in the entries concerning the Elijah and Elisha cycle of stories are noted similar stories about Jesus in the Christian Bible (New Testament). In general, it is clear that Elijah's and Elisha's miracles, multiplication of food, and the raising of the dead accounts influence the same types of stories about Jesus in the gospels.

## PRESUPPOSITIONS

THE HEBREW BIBLE (OLD Testament) accounts of Elijah and Elisha begin as stories passed on by word of mouth from one person to another. Sometime during the oral transmission stage the (deuteronomist) historian, the author of the First Book of Kings and the Second Book of Kings, decides to collect them and write them. A change occurs immediately. One does not tell a story the same way one writes a story. Repetition and correction occur in oral story-telling. Except for future emendations by copyists, single statements by characters and plot structure guides dominate written stories. Furthermore, in both oral and written story-telling, types or models are employed. As already noted, Elijah is a type of Moses; Elisha is a type of Elijah. When orally narrating or writing a story, the teller or author consciously creates one character as a type of another in order to make the character and his words and actions intelligible to the hearer or reader.

The written narratives concerning Elijah and Elisha have been placed by the historian in the First Book of Kings and the Second Book of Kings where the prophets' ministry intersects with the kings of Israel. The historian collects the oral tales about the prophets and decides that the best place to preserve them is next to the kings with whom the prophets associate. Doing this clearly disrupts the narrative form of the rest of the two books about the kings of Israel and Judah. Thus, the Elijah and Elisha narratives represent some of the events in the ministry of those two prophets that were known to the historian through oral tradition. Probably, there were more. As the historian repeats over thirty times about kings, there existed other books named the *Book of the Annals of the Kings of Israel* (1 Kgs 22:39; 2 Kgs 1:18; etc.) and the *Book of the Annals of the Kings of Judah* (1 Kgs 22:45; 2 Kgs 8:23; etc.). More tales may have been recorded about Elijah and Elisha in those books, but neither of those tomes is extant today.

In the Christian Bible (New Testament), the oldest gospel is Mark's account of Jesus' victory. The author of Matthew's Gospel copied and shortened about eighty percent of Mark's material into his book and then added other stories to make the work longer. The author of Luke's Gospel copied and shortened about fifty percent of Mark's material into his orderly account and then added other stories to make the work much longer. Mark's Gospel begins as oral story-telling, lasting for about forty years in that form. An unidentified author, called Mark for the sake of convenience, collects the oral stories, sets a plot, and writes the first gospel around 70 CE. Because Jesus was expected to return soon, no one had thought about recording what he had said and done until Mark came along and realized that he was not returning as quickly as had been thought. About ten years after Mark finished his gospel, Matthew needed to adopt Mark's narrative—originally intended for a peasant Gentile readership—to a Jewish audience. And about twenty years after Mark finished his gospel, Luke needed to adapt Mark's poor Gentile intended work for a rich, upper class, urban, Gentile readership. The author of John's Gospel did not know the existence of the other three works collectively named gospels.

Furthermore, gospels were not first intended to be read privately as is done today. They were meant to be heard in a group. The very low rate of literacy in the first century would have never dictated many copies of texts since most people could not read and their standard practice was to listen to another read the stories to them. Thus, what began as oral story-telling passed on by word of mouth became written story-telling preserved in gospels. A careful reading of Mark's Gospel will reveal the orality still embedded in the text, especially evident in the repetition of words and the organization of stories in three parts. In rewriting Mark, Matthew and Luke remove the last traces of oral story-telling.

Introduction

## ORGANIZATION OF THIS BOOK

In two chapters, there are forty-four entries, the focus of which is contemplation leading to activity and back to contemplation. Each of the forty-forty entries consists of six parts.

1. **Title:** The name of a story featuring the prophet Elijah or Elisha begins the entry.

2. **Scripture**: A few verses or sentences from a biblical text are provided. The text highlights the event under consideration in the entry and illustrates the theme. Except for the last entry in each chapter, the biblical text comes from the First Book of Kings or the Second Book of Kings in the Hebrew Bible (Old Testament). The last entry in each chapter comes from the Old Testament (Apocrypha) Book of Sirach.

3. **Read**: The reader is directed to find the Scripture text in his or her Bible in order to understand the context and to experience the entire biblical story. While the biblical text can be difficult to understand at times, the author has retold it in contemporary English parlance and added other important information in order to help the reader understand it in the reflection. Nevertheless, reading the biblical text gives the reader an experience of it. The author has employed the New Revised Standard Version of the Bible throughout this book, but most biblical translations will work.

4. **Reflection**: A reflection follows the biblical text. The reflection represents the author's contemplation. Reflection is what one should do after the occurrence of any significant event in his or her life. Some, if not all, experiences of life define the individual's spirituality. Through contemplation, a person attempts to recapture life's defining experiences in order to unpack their meaning. The reflections in this book also present some of the context for the biblical text, attempting to surface its meaning, along with other references to the topic in other biblical sources.

   The role of the prophets Elijah and Elisha is to listen attentively to the word of the LORD and contemplate what they hear. Thus, when the prophet speaks, he does not proclaim his own message, but he delivers God's message to his people. In order to get the

## Introduction

LORD's word heard, the prophet deconstructs, that is, he disconnects people from their preconceptions. Thus, the reflection unpacks the Scripture text in light of its prophetic announcer.

The reflection also demonstrates the dialectic of contemplation leading to activity and back to contemplation. It concludes with the author's suggestions as to how the reader might apply the biblical truth about contemplation and activity emerging from the story. The reflection is designed to get the reader to stop and consider the wondrous works of God in the prophets Elijah and Elisha in the hope of also recognizing them today in himself or herself.

5. **Journal/Meditation**: The reflection is followed by a section with questions for journaling and/or personal meditation. The questions function as guides for personal appropriation of the message of the reflection, thus leading the reader into journaling and/or personal meditation. Since the reader knows his or her life better than anyone else, he or she connects his or her life to the reflection in order to delve deeper into contemplation.

    The journal/meditation questions are designed to foster a process of actively applying the reflection to one's life. Out of contemplation one recognizes the action he or she needs to take. In other words, contemplation leads to transformation. Paradox is discovered when seemingly opposite ideas merge together. Light and dark coexist; death and life are one; loss and victory are present simultaneously; and imperfection and perfection are discovered at the same time in the same person.

    This author highly recommends journaling, either written in a notebook or in some electronic format. Seeing one's written thoughts not only objectifies them, but reviewing them engenders deeper contemplation. The questions get one started; where the journaling/meditation goes cannot be predetermined. It may be a single statement or an idea with which one lingers for a few minutes, a few hours, or a few days. The process has no end; the reader decides when he or she has finished exploring the topic because he or she needs to attend to other things.

    The journaling/meditation exercise is best accomplished in quiet, silence, and solitude. All distractions—cell phones, radios, TV, etc.—need to be silenced so one can hear as purely as possible.

# INTRODUCTION

Any kind of contaminants prohibit contemplatively hearing the word of the LORD; if one doesn't hear the LORD's words, he or she cannot act on them.

6. **Prayer**: A prayer concludes the entry and summarizes the original theme announced in the title, presented in the Scripture, read in the Bible, explored in the reflection, and contemplated in the journal/meditation questions. Prayer makes the entire entry thrive. It is the spiritual connection between the reader and God. Out of prayerful contemplation arises activity which sends one back to deeper contemplation.

## SPIRITUALITY

The word *spirituality* is formed from the word *spirit*. It means the fact or condition of being spirit, and it refers to that aspect each person shares—that invisible nature some call soul, being, essence, breath, wind, etc. Since all people participate in the spirit that animates all—a universal spirit—a spiritual process of divine discernment results from connecting the individual spirit through contemplation to the universal Spirit all share. Out of contemplation there flows awareness of what action one needs to take. The experience of activity then sends one back to deeper contemplation. Two biblical models of this process worthy of imitation are the prophets Elijah and Elisha.

# 1

## Elijah

# From Contemplation to Action
## ELIJAH APPEARS

**Scripture**: "... Elijah the Tishbite of Tishbe in Gilead, said to Ahab, 'As the LORD the God of Israel lives, before whom I stand, there shall be neither dew nor rain these years, except by my word.'" (1 Kgs 17:1)

**Read**: 1 Kings 17:1

**Reflection**: Elijah, whose name means *El (God) is Yahweh* or *Yahweh is my God* or *God is my Strength*, is a double entendre, that is, it refers to a middle-ninth-century BCE prophet, and it simultaneously proclaims the message of the prophet: God is the LORD. Elijah's home town, Tishbe in Gilead, is located in the region of Naphtali in Northern Israel. The king of Israel is Ahab, married to Jezebel—daughter of Ethbaal of Tyre in Sidon—who fostered the worship of the Canaanite god Baal in Israel. Thus, both Elijah's name and opening line pit the LORD (Yahweh), Israel's God, against Baal, a fertility god. A battle between the LORD and Baal will determine who the real God of all life is, for without rain all life perishes.

The prophet Elijah, who stands before the LORD, suddenly makes his first appearance in the Bible in the first verse of chapter 17 of the First Book of Kings. He is identified merely as the Tishbite of Tishbe in Gilead. No names of his parents, siblings, or other background are given. He appears to King Ahab of Israel to announce that it will not rain unless he, an agent of the LORD, declares it to take place. In other words, Elijah decrees a drought. Also, he makes it perfectly clear that it is the LORD who controls the elements, and, therefore, fertility!

While the reader is surprised to find Elijah's appearance in a sacred text suddenly, biblical scholars postulate that the author of the First Book of Kings has incorporated the stories concerning Elijah from another source and placed them in the First Book of Kings where tales about King Ahab, Elijah's nemesis, appear. Elijah's sudden appearance, seemingly out of nowhere, is not all that unusual when thought about.

Everyone unexpectedly appears on the world's stage. While birth may have been foreseen for nine months, give or take a few weeks or days, one's human appearance is still sudden, often preceded by only a few contractions of one's mother. Through the birth canal one emerges, tossed into a world with no consultation whatsoever! A career takes off with a bang of a good experience. For example, one's first article is published, one's first book is written, one's first contact is made with an employer, one's first speech is given, one's first class is taught. Whatever becomes a life-changing event affects one because he or she appeared suddenly and unexpectedly and was ready to take advantage of the experience. Some say it is being in the right place at the right time. Elijah would say that it is the LORD's good place and good time that makes the difference.

While modern readers expect to begin almost everything with a positive impression, Elijah abruptly enters the picture and begins with a confrontation. First, the prophet confronts the king. Second, through Elijah, the LORD confronts Baal. And third, Elijah confronts the queen. Expeditiously, Elijah comes out of solitude to action, hopefully to lead those in action to solitude to recognize Israel's true God. In other words, out of his contemplation of the LORD, Elijah will lead those actively worshiping Baal to solitudinous recognition of Israel's God, the LORD.

**Journal/Meditation**: What was the defining moment or break in your career? Was it sudden? How did it change your life? Was God involved in it? How?

**Prayer**: LORD, my strength, out of my solitude bring action that I may serve you all the days of my life. You are God forever and ever. Amen.

## WATER AND FOOD

**Scripture**: "The word of the LORD came to [Elijah], saying, . . . 'You shall drink from the wadi, and I have commanded the ravens to feed you there.'" (1 Kgs 17:2, 4)

**Read**: 1 Kings 17:2–7

**Reflection**: Elijah has spoken but one sentences about a drought, and the LORD directs him to the Wadi Cherith, east of the Jordan River in the land of Israel. A wadi is a stream bed which may contain water at some times and be dry at other times. While the rest of the land experiences drought, God provides the water of life along with bread and meat to his prophet. The paradox is not to be missed: In the midst of emptiness the LORD provides abundance both in the morning and in the afternoon! Elijah is camped alone near the wadi, and he is dependent upon God alone for life.

Contemplation occurs when one is alone with God. Elijah appears out of contemplation, declares a drought, and immediately returns to solitude. The word of the LORD that comes to him sends him back to seclusion, where, in the midst of drought he has water, and, having nothing, ravens provide him with bread and meat two times a day! A further paradox exists here. Ravens are notoriously voracious, but they bring bread and meat to the prophet instead of devouring it themselves. However, in due time the wadi dries because the LORD has declared through Elijah that it would not rain until Elijah said it would, and the LORD had not yet brought the drought to an end.

This short story of Elijah finding water and being provided with bread and meat is meant to parallel the similar account of God providing water from the rock for the Israelites (Exod 17:1–7) and before that bread from heaven (Exod 16:3–8) and quail (Exod 16:9–18) through Moses. Repeatedly, throughout the narrative about Elijah, the LORD treats the prophet in a way similar to how he treated Moses and provides words and deeds that parallel the words and deeds of Moses.

Dependence is not a word most people like; most people prefer the word independence. Dependence, reliance upon the LORD for support, trusting that God will provide, implies openness to the LORD's will. Such dependence makes Elijah vulnerable, but it also opens him to being an instrument of God's will, a minister of God's deeds. Furthermore, the LORD hides Elijah from King Ahab. He protects and preserves him for the mission God has in mind for him. There is more of the story to tell.

This is true for all who embrace Elijah's stance of dependency upon God, realizing that it is not their story that is unfolding, but it is God's story unfolding in and through their lives. In the Christian Bible (New Testament), the Letter of James calls Elijah's proclamation of the drought a prayer. The author of the letter states that the prayer of a righteous person is powerful and effective. "Elijah was a human being like us," writes James, "and he prayed fervently that it might not rain, and for three years and six months it did not rain on the earth. Then he prayed again, and the heaven gave rain and the earth yielded its harvest" (Jas 5:17–18). Effective prayer wells up out of contemplation because it is prompted by the LORD, who then sees that it becomes effective.

**Journal/Meditation**: Upon whom are you dependent? What feelings does the word *dependence* spark in you? How are dependence upon God and prayer connected? Do you find paradox in your life like Elijah did? Does it lead you to deeper contemplation?

**Prayer:** In the midst of emptiness, you provide abundance, O LORD. Teach me dependence upon you alone that out of my solitude your words may be heard and your deeds made known now and forever and ever. Amen.

# Elijah

## ZAREPHATH

**Scripture:** Elijah said to the widow: ". . . [T]hus says the LORD the God of Israel: The jar of meal will not be emptied and the jug of oil will not fail until the day that the LORD sends rain on the earth.'" (1 Kgs 17:14)

**Read:** 1 Kings 17:8–16

**Reflection:** Once the wadi dries, the LORD sends Elijah to Zarephath in Sidon. Modern Bible readers will not recognize that Sidon is outside of Israel, nor will they notice that the LORD is sending his prophet to Baal's territory, Phoenician land, to demonstrate that Israel's LORD is greater than Baal and God of all people. The paradox gets even better; the prophet is sent to one of the most powerless of people: a widow, who is starving! She has no man to provide for her, and the provisions she has are almost exhausted. Even in her poverty, however, she, a non-Israelite, is willing to serve Israelite Elijah with a vessel of water and her last morsel of bread.

The author of Luke's Gospel in the Christian Bible (New Testament) recognized this paradox in his unique presentation of Jesus' first discourse in the Nazareth synagogue. The Lukan Jesus proves that no prophet is accepted in the prophet's hometown by reminding his listeners that "there were many widows in Israel in the time of Elijah, when the heaven was shut up three years and six months, and there was a sever famine over all the land; yet Elijah was sent to none of them except to a widow at Zarephath in Sidon" (Luke 4:25-26). In Luke's Gospel, some people even begin rumors "that Elijah had appeared" (Luke 9:8) in the person of Jesus, and Jesus' disciples report that some think that he is Elijah (Luke 9:19).

All the widow has is a handful of meal in a jar and a little oil in a jug. Once she gathers a few sticks to bake the meal and oil into bread, she and her son will eat it and die. Elijah exhorts her—who has just acknowledged the LORD as Elijah's God—not to fear using the remainder of her supplies. The LORD has another plan: The jar of meal will not empty, and the jug of oil will not run dry until the LORD sends rain on the earth. Again, Elijah's words and deeds are modeled on those of Moses in the Hebrew Bible (Old Testament) Book of Numbers. The abundance of manna (Num 11:7–9) and quail (Num 11:31–32) provided by the LORD through Moses is seen again in the abundance of meal and oil provided by the LORD through Elijah.

In the midst of famine, there is plenty. God's world, Elijah knows, is one of plenty. Elijah is a minister of plenty. This world is one of famine. There is never enough food, water, health care, guns, gas, oil, etc. so one must hoard. Elijah instills plenty into the widow of Zarephath. He tells her to share what little she has and watch the resulting abundance. Here, a non-Israelite—and a widow at that!—obeys Elijah's God. In contrast, the Israelites, who are following Baal, are in drought. Out of scarcity and poverty, there come plenty and abundance. Out of solitude is born a miracle.

Contemplation and action are united in Elijah. The mystic moment of abundance puts together things that form a whole only on a deeper level. The widow goes to that unified place—spirituality—where only God keeps meal and oil in a steady supply. This miracle is an event with which human comprehension has not yet caught up to divine activity. Elijah leads the widow into a not-yet-chartered human realm where surrendered spirit becomes an instrument of the LORD's abundance. Furthermore, this narrative illustrates that God's care for people is universal; he is God even of non-Israelites, non-Jews, biblically referred to as Gentiles.

**Journal/Meditation:** In what experience of your life did scarcity and poverty become plenty and abundance? How were contemplation and action united? What were the meal and oil that came abundantly to you? How was God demonstrating universal care for people?

**Prayer:** As once you did for the widow of Zarephath, O LORD, multiply my meager resources so they become an abundance of life to be shared with others. I surrender myself to you now and forever. Amen.

## REVIVED SON

**Scripture:** Elijah "stretched himself upon the child [of the widow of Zarephath] three times, and cried out to the LORD, 'O LORD my God, let his child's life come into him again.'" (1 Kgs 17:21)

**Read:** 1 Kings 17:17–24

**Reflection:** Breath indicates life. Because breath has left the son of the widow of Zarephath—now referred to as the mistress of the house—he is dead. The widow is now even more powerless. Truly, she has no man in her life to provide for her! She concludes that her son's death is divine punishment due to some unknown sin. However, Elijah knows this is not how the LORD treats those who believe in him.

Elijah opens himself in solitude to being the vehicle for life, breath, or spirit. He removes the body of the dead boy from his mother's arms and carries him to an upper room—a guest room—where Elijah is staying. This upper room is on the roof; in a three-storied universe, it is as close as Elijah can get on the middle story to the upper story, where God lives. The prophet lays the boy on his own bed, itself a place of death and life. Every night people enter into the sleep of death on a bed and awaken the next day to new life. In the solitude of his room, Elijah places the breathless boy on his bed and asks God why the boy died, but his question is not answered. So, knowing the divine number three—indicating divine presence—the prophet stretches himself upon the child three times, praying that the LORD will let the child's life—breath—return. The life—breath—goes from Elijah to the boy, making the prophet a vehicle for life. God hears Elijah's prayer, and the child revives, beginning to breathe again. As will be seen, the prophet Elisha also stretches himself upon a dead child and restores breath to him (2 Kgs 4:34–35). While he does not stretch himself upon Eutychus, Paul picks up the dead man who had fallen from three—divine presence—floors above and declares that his life breath is still in him (Acts 20:9–12). This account, written by the same author who wrote Luke's Gospel, uses that story to echo the account of Jesus telling Jairus that his daughter was not dead but sleeping (Luke 8:41–42a, 49–56); Luke rewrote this narrative that he found in Mark's Gospel (5:22–24a, 35–43) in order to focus on Jesus' power over death and life.

Elijah re-enacts the LORD God's deed of breathing into the first man's nostrils the breath of life so that he became a living being (Gen 2:7). The prophet Ezekiel narrates how the LORD told him to prophesy to the breath over the valley of dry bones: "Thus says the Lord GOD: Come from the four winds, O breath, and breathe upon these slain, that they may live" (Ezek 37:9). Of course, the breath came into them, just like it did for the widow's son. Unique to Luke's Gospel is the story of Jesus bringing back to life the son of the widow of Nain (Luke 7:11–16). All Jesus does in order to restore breath to the dead man is to touch the bier upon which he is being carried to his grave and call him to rise. The response of those witnessing this event is the declaration that a great prophet has risen among them. There is little doubt that Luke modeled his account on that of Elijah's restoration of the widow's son. In restoring sons to their widowed mothers, both Elijah and Jesus restore life to the widows because they need their sons for their livelihoods.

After Elijah demonstrates the LORD's power over life and death in Baal's land, he returns the boy to his widowed mother, and she declares him to be a man of God who has the word of the LORD in his mouth. This is quiet a declaration for a non-Jewish woman to make! A Baalist woman confesses the LORD's power at work through Elijah! What a paradox! Not only is this story a demonstration of God's universal care for all people, but it presents the prophet as a spiritual power broker, an empty contemplative vessel for the LORD to fill with action. Again, contemplation and action merge. Elijah is the steady, centered, poised, rooted prophet who takes the boy to his private room and asks God to restore the cycle of life. Not only is the boy restored, but his mother is restored, too. Out of contemplation comes action, and out of action comes more contemplation.

Today, ventilators, oxygen masks, oxygen pumps, and other types of equipment continue the transpiration of life. Some people may be quick to dismiss these as scientific medical devices and achievements, but they may be the way the LORD restores the breath of life today.

**Journal/Meditation:** How have you experienced the union of death and life? How have you experience the breath of life? When have you been dead and someone became the vehicle for the restoration of your life? What action has come out of your contemplation?

**Prayer:** O LORD, let the life that you once breathed into your creation come into people again that they may rise from death to be revived in your presence. You are God forever and ever. Amen.

## THE PLAN: PART 1

**Scripture:** "Elijah said [to Obadiah], 'As the LORD of hosts lives, before whom I stand, I will surely show myself to [King Ahab] today.'" (1 Kgs 18:15)

**Read:** 1 Kings 18:1–16

**Reflection:** Three years have elapsed since Elijah announced the beginning of the drought. The note that the Israelites are in the third year of the drought indicates that it is a divinely caused and controlled event. The prophet has been in solitude, but he hears God's word sending him out of his contemplative location with the widow of Zarephath and her son to King Ahab of Israel who has sought Elijah all during the lack of rain: "Go present yourself to Ahab; I will send rain on the earth" (1 Kgs 18:1).

Enter Obadiah, whose name means *servant of the LORD*, chief steward of Ahab. The paradox of the LORD's servant being in charge of the wicked king's palace should not be missed. Obadiah demonstrates his loyalty to God by hiding the LORD's prophets in caves in groups of fifty and supplying them with bread and water in order to save their lives from Jezebel, Ahab's wife. Obadiah does for the LORD's prophets what the widow had done for Elijah. While Obadiah is hiding the LORD's prophets behind the king's and queen's back, he is instructed by Ahab to seek water and grass to keep the horses and mules alive while the drought continues to last. Ahab is concerned about horses and mules, while Obadiah is concerned about God's servants being killed by Jezebel! It is obvious which one has discerned the divine plan!

Elijah finds Obadiah and tells him that he is ready to confront Ahab, who has sought for Elijah relentlessly. Obadiah fears telling Ahab that Elijah is present; in the past when such an announcement was made, the spirit of the LORD carried away Elijah. If this happens again, Obadiah fears that Ahab will do to him what Jezebel has done to God's prophets. Obadiah, it seems, is a good man in a bad place! Using the same language about standing before the LORD as he did earlier (1 Kgs 17:1) when announcing the drought, Elijah calms Obadiah's fear by telling him that he intends to see Ahab that very day.

With the three-year drought the LORD of hosts has demonstrated that he is the supreme fertility God. Furthermore, he has assured Elijah that it is all in God's good time when the rain will come. Elijah is like Moses, who waited for the LORD to act (Exod 24:12). Similarly, there are moments in life that are labeled special, such as a graduation, a marriage, a birth of a child, etc. These special moments in people's lives are also important in God's life. The divine plan is further revealed and brought another step to completion through them. People don't often make this connection because they are too busy enacting their own plan to realize that it also may be a small part of the divine plan. The divine plan is unfolding before their eyes, just as it was for Obadiah and Elijah.

**Journal/Meditation:** What special moments in your life may be special moments in God's life that further his plan? Like Obadiah, have you ever had to appear serving one person when you were really countering his or her action? Why is it important to contemplate your actions which lead to further contemplation?

**Prayer:** LORD of hosts, I stand before you this day revering you greatly and realizing that I am a part of your plan. Grant that I may be your servant now and forever. Amen.

From Contemplation to Action

## THE PLAN: PART 2

**Scripture:** Elijah said to Ahab, "Now therefore have all Israel assemble for me at Mount Carmel, with the four hundred fifty prophets of Baal and the four hundred prophets of Asherah, who eat at Jezebel's table." (1 Kgs 18:19)

**Read:** 1 Kings 18:17–20

**Reflection**: Elijah approaches King Ahab, who calls the prophet the troubler of Israel, just as the widow of Zarephath had addressed him upon the death of her son (1 Kgs 17:18) and as Ahab will refer to him again later in the story (1 Kgs 21:20). In other words, Ahab (874–853 BCE) blames Elijah for the three-year drought, like the widow blamed him for the death of her son and Ahab will blame him for having discovered Ahab's crime. However, Elijah, the disturber of the usual peace, declares that it is Ahab's apostasy—forsaking the LORD's commandments and following Baal—that has troubled Israel. Elijah confronts Ahab's sin by simultaneously referring to the sky and fertility god Baal and the local fertility gods that manifest him, the Baals.

In this second part of the plan, the prophet Elijah takes the initiative away from King Ahab. Elijah, who stands before the LORD, assumes the power to tell Ahab what to do. First, he is instructed to assemble Baal's four hundred fifty prophets and Asherah's (Baal's goddess consort) four hundred prophets—all of whom are fed by Jezebel—on Mount Carmel. Second, he is to have all Israel assemble there also. Obediently, Ahab summons all the Israelites and the eight hundred fifty prophets to Mount Carmel, meaning *orchard* or *vineyard* of El. The name El means *God* in Semitic languages. Paradoxically, Elijah—whose name means *the LORD is God*—chooses a fertility site—vineyard or orchard—to demonstrate who the real fertility God is and defeat Baal's and Asherah's adherents on their own ground!

Again, Elijah looks like Moses, who summoned the Israelite assembly at Mount Horeb (Sinai) to witness the divine fire and seal the covenant (Exod 19:1–24:18). Elijah instructs Ahab to gather the Israelites on Mount Carmel, where they will witness the fire and renew the covenant. Just as the Horeb (Sinai) assembly was no contest for the LORD's fire, neither will this one be on Mount Carmel. Ahab's acting according to Elijah's instructions already indicates who the real fertility God is: the LORD, before whom his prophet, Elijah, stands!

The classic one prophet of the LORD versus eight hundred fifty prophets of Baal and Asherah adds drama to the story. Even a modern reader is moved to side with the LORD's lone prophet. Today, he is the man or woman who stands alone against uncountable odds to disclose the illegal practices of a company, the racism that dictates who gets a job and who does not, the lies told by another to cover money-laundering, etc. Elijah is everyone who stands for integrity, justice, righteousness, and truth. He, who stands before the LORD, trusts that God will vindicate him.

**Journal/Meditation**: When have you been labeled a trouble-maker? Were you making trouble or standing for a treasured value or virtue? Explain. Have you ever had an experience of standing alone before the LORD? What did you learn from it?

**Prayer**: You never abandon those who stand before you, O LORD. Strengthen me in your service today and every day now and forever and ever. Amen.

## TERMS OF THE CONTEST

**Scripture**: "Elijah then came near to all the people, and said, 'How long will you go limping with two different opinions? If the LORD is God, follow him; but if Baal, then follow him.'" (1 Kgs 18:21)

**Read**: 1 Kings 18:21–24

**Reflection**: Once all the participants are assembled on Mount Carmel, Elijah asks them how long two different positions will be kept on the table. The people, according to Elijah, keep hopping from one leg to another in their effort to determine who is God. They keep straddling the fence. In order to settle the question once for all, Elijah presents the terms of the contest. From Elijah's point of view, it is very simple: If the LORD is God, then the people should follow him; but if Baal is god, then the people should follow him. However, no one answers Elijah's question about who is the real God. Not a word is spoken because it is easier not to give an answer than it is to take a position and end up on the wrong side!

Elijah, who has a flare for drama, claims to be the only prophet of God left; he must have forgotten about the one hundred prophets saved by Obadiah (1 Kgs 18:3–4)! Elijah is overstating his case in order to emphasize the seriousness of his question. His aloneness may be due to him being the only prophet of the LORD on Mount Carmel, and it may refer to his solitude, out of which he acts. Nevertheless, he explains how the contest will take shape. Two bulls will be brought forward. The prophets of Baal will choose one, and the other will be given to Elijah. Not only is a bull a very strong fertility sign, but it is bulls' blood that Moses used to sprinkle the Israelites at the covenant renewal ceremony before Mount Horeb (Sinai) (Exod 24:5–8). As seen before, the character of Elijah is modeled on that of Moses.

The directions given by Elijah are simple. The bull is to be cut into pieces which are placed on wood to be lit on fire. Elijah will prepare the other bull. The god who answers with fire, that is, the god who ignites the wood under the cut-in-pieces bull, will reveal who the real God is! Some might accuse Elijah of cheating, because he is very familiar with the LORD's descent upon Mount Horeb (Sinai) as fire (Exod 19:18; 24:17) and lightning (Exod 19:16), fire in the sky. With the rules of the contest voiced, the attendees declare, "Well spoken" (1 Kgs 18:24).

Of particular importance in this narrative is Elijah's coming near to the people (1 Kgs 18:21). Later in the story he will invite the people to come closer (1 Kgs 18:30), and he himself will come near (1 Kgs 18:36). The three notices about coming near or drawing closer are meant to awaken the people to the immanence of the LORD. The divine presence is clearly indicated by these three occurrences.

**Journal/Meditation**: When have you experience the divine presence? What sign(s) indicated it to you? Did your awareness of the divine presence enable you to act? Have you ever experienced yourself alone in any way like Elijah and you knew that God was with you?

**Prayer**: O LORD, you are God revealing your presence as fire and lightning. Make me aware of your nearness today, tomorrow, and forever. Amen.

## NO ANSWER

**Scripture**: "As midday passed, [the prophets of Baal] raved on until the time of the offering of the oblation, but there was no voice, no answer, and no response." (1 Kgs 18:29)

**Read**: 1 Kings 18:25–29

**Reflection**: There is no doubt that Elijah is in charge of the contest between him and the prophets of Baal. The prophet instructs Baal's prophets to prepare the bull by cutting it into pieces and putting it on wood. Then, they are to call on the name of their god without setting the wood on fire. They do as Elijah instructs and call upon Baal from morning to noon, but they hear no voice and they get no answer to their petition as they hop around the altar of wood with pieces of bull on it.

Elijah, who knows who the real God is, mocks the hundreds of Baal's prophets. He tells them to cry louder because Baal may not be able to hear them. He may be meditating. Maybe he has wandered away. Maybe he has taken a journey. Maybe he is asleep and needs to be awakened. Baal's prophets even slash their extremities with swords so that blood gushes over them in order to prompt a response from Baal. Their feverish dancing and blood-letting, magic-like trance continues until around three in the afternoon when it is determined that no voice will be heard, no answer will be given, and no response will be forthcoming.

Instead of the blood of bulls that Moses sprinkled upon the Israelites at the Mount Horeb (Sinai) covenant renewal ceremony (Exod 24:8), signifying a fertile relationship of life between God and people, the prophets of Baal's shedding of blood ratifies their death in two ways. First, they are killing themselves by their blood-letting, and second, they will be put to death at the end of the contest. The future can be guaranteed only by the LORD.

**Journal/Meditation**: Who guarantees your future? In what experience of your life have you encountered infertile gods? Did you mock them like Elijah did?

**Prayer**: Life-giving LORD, you enter into relationship with people to give them abundance. Grant me the grace to know the fullness of life in your presence now and forever and ever. Amen.

## PREPARING A THEOPHANY

**Scripture**: "At the time of the offering of the oblation, the prophet Elijah came near and said, 'O LORD, God of Abraham, Isaac, and Israel, let it be known this day that you are God in Israel, that I am your servant, and that I have done all these things at your biding.' Then the fire of the LORD fell and consumed the burnt offering, the wood, the stones, and the dust, and even licked up the water that was in the trench." (1 Kgs 18:36, 38)

**Read**: 1 Kings 18:30–40

**Reflection**: Elijah looks the most like Moses when he prepares for the theophany—God's appearance in visible form—that ultimately takes place. Like Moses builds an altar and erects twelve pillars to represent the twelve tribes of Israel (Exod 24:4b), Elijah takes twelve stones, representing the tribes of Jacob, and builds an altar (1 Kgs 18:30b–32a). The prophet then digs a trench around the altar, deep enough to hold about five gallons of water. After assembling the wood on the altar, Elijah cuts the bull (that the prophets of Baal did not choose) into pieces and places them on the altar. Then, employing the sacred number four, indicating the earth, and three, indicating the divine, he instructs that four jars be filled with water three times and poured over the offering, re-emphasizing the sacred number twelve. Later in the narrative, Elisha, Elijah's successor, will be found plowing with twelve yoke of oxen (1 Kgs 19:19) to further emphasize the foundational unity of the Kingdom of Israel in the North and the Kingdom of Judah in the South.

At a time of drought, the water represents a priceless libation, but it hints at the abundant rain that is about to end the three-year divine drought. Elijah's prayer not only names Israel's God as the LORD, but mentions the divine three predecessors: Abraham, Isaac, and Israel (Jacob), just like Moses does (Exod 32:13). Furthermore, there are three petitions to Elijah's prayer: that God let it be known that he is God in Israel, that Elijah is his servant, and that Elijah is doing what the LORD has instructed him to do. His final petition is that God will win the contest and turn back the hearts of his people to him.

Throughout this narrative, Elijah has been listening to the word of the LORD telling him what God wants done. Out of contemplation the prophet hears the divine voice, and then he acts on it, as he is doing in this scene. Out of contemplation emerges action. Like a tuning fork used to prepare a piano for playing, Elijah is in tune with the LORD. They resonate together.

Thus, it is no surprise to Elijah that the LORD's fire—lightning—falls from the sky and consumes the bull, the wood, the stones, the dust, and licks up the water in the trench. Elijah is another Moses, who witnesses the appearance of the glory of the LORD as a devouring fire on the top of Mount Horeb (Sinai) (Exod 24:17). Elijah is the minister, the agent, of the theophany. Once the theophany is finished, the people of Israel fall on their faces and declare the winner of the contest: "The LORD indeed is God" (1Kgs 18:39).

All that remains is for the people to seize Baal's prophets and put them to death. This action imitates Queen Jezebel's action of slaughtering the LORD's prophets (1 Kgs 18:13), as reported earlier by Obadiah. It is not an accident that the death of four hundred fifty prophets takes place in the Wadi Kishon, a stream bed which may or may not have water in it depending on the time of the year. It will not be long before the drought is ended; the blood of Baal's prophets running in the dry stream bed predicts the abundant life-giving rain that will fall a few verses later. Furthermore,

Elijah's direction that the prophets of Baal be killed makes him look like Moses, who ordered the Levites to kill three thousand people who had worshiped the golden calf (Exod 32:25–28).

**Journal/Meditation**: How is water precious to you? Do you conserve it? Do you consider it a divine gift? What are your sacred numbers? Have you ever experienced God's presence as fire? Explain. How does your prayer indicate that you are in tune with God?

**Prayer**: O LORD, God of Abraham, Isaac, and Israel, let it be known this day that you are God of all the earth, that I am your servant, and that I am in tune with your will. Answer me that others may know you, O LORD, and that you have turned their hearts toward you. Amen.

## END OF DROUGHT

**Scripture**: "In a little while the heavens grew black with clouds and wind; there was a heavy rain." (1 Kgs 18:45a)

**Read**: 1 Kings 18:41–46

**Reflection**: Before Elijah announces the end of the drought and oncoming rain, he tells King Ahab to leave Mount Carmel and feast, another element of a theophany. Elijah's directive about eating and drinking is meant to echo the eating and drinking of Moses and Aaron, Nadab, and Abihu and seventy elders before the LORD on Mount Horeb (Sinai) (Exod 24:9–11). While Ahab goes to eat and drink, Elijah goes to the top of Mount Carmel, just like Moses went to the top of Mount Horeb (Sinai) (Exod 19:20; 24:2, 9, 12, 15). On Mount Carmel, Elijah takes the position of prayer, bowing before the LORD and placing his face between his knees so that he dare not look at God, again imitating Moses (Exod 3:6).

As a man of God, Elijah sends his unnamed servant to look toward the sea, but the servant reports seeing no cloud. Then, employing the sacred number seven (the sum of three, indicating the divine, and four, indicating the earth), he sends the servant to look seven times. The rain falls from the heavens (three) to the earth (four), making the earth fertile! Upon searching the sky the seventh time, the servant reports seeing a little cloud rising from the sea. Just like Moses brought forth water from a rock (Exod 17:6), Elijah announces a heavy rain from a small cloud. It is not long before the real fertility God manifests himself again with black clouds in the heavens, wind, and a heavy rain.

King Ahab gets into his chariot and rushes off to Jezreel to avoid being caught in the thunderstorm. However, Elijah lifts up his clothes and runs ahead of the king to the entrance of Jezreel, seventeen miles from Mount Carmel! God's hand—power—is on Elijah, whose name means *God is my Strength*. Indeed, as the reader has seen, the LORD's strength is given to Elijah in solitude. The prophet is in sync with his God. He has access to strength that is not his own. In the words of the psalmist, he is still before the LORD and waits patiently for him (Ps 37:7a). Out of his contemplation, Elijah acts with divine power.

Awareness of the presence of God empowers the prophet. Awareness of the divine presence can empower people today. Running seventeen miles and beating a chariot to the city gates is an extraordinary feat, but daily access to God's power in solitude can fuel a runner's high, a walker's solitary prayer, a friend's or spouse's grace, love, or energy. The hand of the LORD is stretched out over those who wish to access the strength it contains.

**Journal/Meditation**: What is your prayer position? What great feat have you brought forth from your prayer? How have you experienced God's hand of power being on you?

**Prayer**: Bowing before you, O LORD, I place my face between my knees because I dare not look upon your face. Send your rain from the heavens to the earth to make it fertile. Send your word to fill my life with your grace now and forever. Amen.

## FLEEING FOR LIFE

**Scripture**: Elijah "was afraid; he got up and fled for his life, and came to Beer-sheba, which belongs to Judah; he left his servant there." (1 Kgs 19:3)

**Read**: 1 Kings 19:1–3

**Reflection**: Once King Ahab gets to Jezreel, he tells his queen, Jezebel, that Elijah has had killed all her prophets of Baal. She responds to the news by sending a messenger to the prophet informing him that she seeks revenge and will see to it that he is dead by the following day! Fearing for his life, Elijah enters into a solitary journey to Beer-sheba (meaning *well of seven* springs), the scene of a theophany both to Isaac (Gen 26:23–25) and Jacob (Gen 46:1–5), a pilgrimage of one hundred thirty miles! Alone, Elijah is ready to discern the next step that the LORD has planned for his life, which he is preserving by escaping Jezebel's net. The prophet has one hundred thirty miles of solitude to determine what God wills for him.

Discernment, the process of seeing or understanding something that is not clear or obvious in spirituality, can occur only when one is free from distractions. Elijah chooses the very biblical process of taking a journey in imitation of Abraham, Isaac, and Jacob. Discernment is difficult to do in a modern world filled with text, tweet, and facebook words. Add in e-mails, internet, and cell phone communications and it is easy to be distracted for hours. TV, video games, tablets, and other forms of noise are barriers to discernment. In Elijah's world, one took a solitary journey to discern God's will. Such a road trip may be necessary today.

It is also important to note at this point in the cycle of Elijah stories that the journey serves as a bridge from one theophany on Mount Carmel to another one on Mount Horeb (Sinai). As has been seen, the prophet Elijah's deeds are modeled on the greatest of the prophets'—Moses'—deeds. In order to complete the conforming of Elijah to the Moses model, Elijah has to get to Mount Horeb (Sinai). From Beer-sheba, where he leaves his servant, Elijah continues his solitary trek into the wilderness toward the mountain of God (Exod 3:1; 24:13).

**Journal/Meditation**: When have you spent time in solitude? Have you ever taken a solitary journey, pilgrimage, or road trip? What did you discover that God willed for you?

**Prayer**: All of my life is a journey in your presence, O LORD. Strengthen me with your grace that I may walk it in your service today, tomorrow, and for as long as I live. Amen.

## UNDER THE BROOM TREE

**Scripture**: Elijah "himself went a day's journey into the wilderness, and came and sat down under a solitary broom tree. He asked that he might die: 'It is enough; now, O LORD, take away my life, for I am no better than my ancestors.'" (1 Kgs 19:4)

**Read**: 1 Kings 19:4–9a

**Reflection**: After winning the contest determining who the real God is in Israel and being threatened with death at the hands of Queen Jezebel, Elijah finds himself very vulnerable. So, after leaving his servant in Beer-sheba, he journeys one day into the wilderness. There, the prophet finds a solitary broom tree, under which he sits. The solitary broom tree in the desert is a mirror of the solitary prophet sitting under it! Elijah is empty of courage; he has poured out all of it on Mount Carmel. From his point of view, he is finished with his life; so he prays that the LORD will take it and remove his prophetic burden. However, just because Elijah thinks that God is finished with him doesn't mean that the LORD is, indeed, done with him.

After he prays, Elijah falls asleep under the broom tree. Sleep is a type of death, and death is for what he prayed. Furthermore, through the tree reaching up to the heavens with its roots stretching down to Sheol, where the dead live in the Hebrew cosmos, the prophet finds himself between death (Sheol) and God (heaven) during the night. Elijah also mirrors the patriarch Jacob, who wrestled with God throughout the night (Gen 32:24–30). In his solitude under the solitary broom tree, Elijah is waiting for death or the LORD's strength; he is letting his heart take courage as he waits for the LORD (Ps 27:14), even though he prays for death!

Waking up suddenly, Elijah feels an angel—God in disguise—touching him and telling him to get up and eat the cake baked on hot stones and the jar of water sitting before him. Before this, ravens brought him bread and meat, and the Wadi Cherith furnished him with water (1 Kgs 17:3–6). And after that, the widow of Zarephath supplied his needs (1 Kgs 17:8–16). After eating and drinking, which will strengthen him for more life in the LORD's service, Elijah lay down again, because he is set on dying. But, as has been seen so many times before in these stories, Elijah is a paradox: While he wishes for death, he eats bread and drinks water! Thus, the death-defying angel of the LORD comes a second time, touches him, and urges him to eat and drink in preparation for the journey to Mount Horeb (Sinai). It is important to note that this is divine food that will keep the prophet walking for forty days and forty nights to Horeb (Sinai), the mountain of God.

The angel of the LORD, who gives Moses food and drink and a mission to Mount Horeb (Sinai), makes Elijah look like Moses, who also received his mission from the angel of the LORD (Exod 3:2). Of course, Elijah's forty-day journey to Mount Horeb (Sinai) also makes him resemble Moses, who led the Israelites through the desert for forty years, all the while eating manna (Exod 16:35). Once he gets to the mountain of the LORD, Elijah enters a cave, where he spends the night. The cave is very much like the cleft in the rock in which the LORD placed Moses when his glory passed by because no one can see God's face and live (Exod 33:20–23).

However, the cave is more than protection for Elijah. The cave is also a burial place, a place to die. Ancient burial practices often involved a cave with shelves carved into the walls upon which were placed bodies wrapped in linen strips. A large round stone was rolled over the cave's entrance. And the cave is a womb, from which Elijah will be raised from the dead to complete his God-given mission on earth. After sleeping and eating under a solitary broom tree and walking in solitude for forty days and nights, the solitary prophet enters into even deeper solitude in a cave. In the protective cave, Elijah contemplates death, while the LORD contemplates new life.

After a day of action, all people need time for contemplation. Such a need for solitude may not parallel the amount of time needed by Elijah, but it is required nevertheless. A man cave, a lady lounge, a workshop, a chapel, a prayer corner, a spa, a sauna, etc. can be the place for contemplative solitude. As Elijah demonstrates, it is also a protected place for death and rejuvenation. The active spiritual live thrives because it is preceded by deep, contemplative solitude.

**Journal/Meditation**: In what situations do you find yourself the most vulnerable? Where do you go for solitary contemplation and rejuvenation? How much time do you need generally? With what does God nourish you while you are there? What angel of the LORD has appeared to you in your cave?

**Prayer:** Some days are enough, O LORD, when I ask you to take away my life for I realize that I am no better than my ancestors. However, your angel brings nourishment during contemplation and rejuvenates me to serve you. I praise you now and forever. Amen.

## SHEER SILENCE

**Scripture:** "Now there was a great wind, so strong that it was splitting mountains and breaking rocks in pieces before the LORD, but the LORD was not in the wind; and after the wind an earthquake, but the LORD was not in the earthquake; and after the earthquake a fire, but the LORD was not in the fire; and after the fire a sound of sheer silence." (1 Kgs 19:11b–12)

**Read**: 1 Kings 19:9b–18

**Reflection:** After spending the night in the contemplative solitude of the cave at Mount Horeb (Sinai), Elijah hears the word of the LORD asking him why he is there. He replies by explaining the situation in Israel: The people have forsaken God's covenant, torn down his altars, and killed his prophets. While Elijah has remained zealous, he has fled from Israel to the mountain because Queen Jezebel is seeking to kill him. As he has done before, Elijah claims to be the only prophet of the LORD left, having forgotten the one hundred Obadiah saved (1 Kgs 18:13), but maybe only calling attention to the fact that he alone sits in the cave on the mountain.

Elijah's contemplative solitude influences the portrayal of Jesus praying alone in the Christian Bible (New Testament). He goes to an unnamed mountain to pray (Mark 6:46), often being alone (Matt 14:23; John 6:15) or with his disciples near him (Luke 9:18). In Luke's Gospel in particular, Jesus is found in prayerful contemplation before every major activity (Luke 3:21, 5:16, 6:12; 9:29; 11:1, 23:34, 46).

After answering the LORD's question, God speaks to Elijah a second time, telling him to go stand on the mountain, just like Moses did multiple times (Exod 19:20; 24:1, 9–10, 12, 15, etc.). God tells Elijah that the LORD is about to pass by. First, Elijah experiences a strong wind, which is the very first element ever mentioned of a biblical theophany (Gen 1:2) and which turns the Sea of Reeds into dry land (Exod 14:21); the LORD is not in the wind. Second, there is an earthquake, like that experienced by Moses on Mount Horeb (Sinai) (Exod 19:18), but the LORD is not in the earthquake. Third, there is fire, like that experienced by Moses on Mount Horeb (Sinai) (Exod 19:18; 24:17), but the LORD is not in the fire. Finally, it is in the sound of sheer silence that God is revealed. It is not in the active, booming thunder, lightning, cloud, fire, smoke, trumpet blast, and earthquake that the divine presence is revealed to Elijah as it was to Moses, but in the sound of gentle, contemplative stillness, which is quite a contrast to the previous manifestation. Silence is God's language; God dwells in silence. It is in being still that Elijah recognizes God (Ps 46:10). He has waited in silence for the LORD (Ps 62:1), and recognizes that the LORD is with him in sheer silence. This silence contains unlimited potentialities; it opens Elijah to the future and the continued presence of his God. Jesus, too, speaks about not being alone because the Father is with him in the silence (John 16:32).

After hearing the sound of a gentle stillness, Elijah wraps his mantle over his face, just like the LORD covers Moses with his hand (Exod 33:22), as God passes by. Once he recognizes that the LORD has passed by, Elijah stands at the entrance to the cave, like Moses stood before the burning bush (Exod 3:1–12) to receive his new commission, his new mandate with its responsibilities. First, however and for a second time, God asks the prophet what he is doing on Mount Horeb (Sinai), and, for the second time using the same words as before, Elijah explains that he has been zealous for the LORD, the God of hosts, but the Israelites have forsaken his covenant, torn down his altars, and killed his prophets. He alone is left, and Queen Jezebel, wife of King Ahab, is seeking his life.

For the third, divine time, the LORD addresses Elijah, giving him a set of directions. He is to anoint Hazael as king over Aram, Jehu as king over Israel, and Elisha as his successor. Also, the LORD tells Elijah that there will be a lot of killing as evil people are cleaned out of the LORD's world. Furthermore, God promises to leave alive seven thousand faithful Israelites who have not knelt to, bowed to, or kissed Baal. As will be seen, Elijah accomplishes only the third part of his mission, namely, anointing Elisha as his prophetic successor.

In his Letter to the Romans, Paul quotes Elijah's spoken words to the LORD on Mount Horeb (Sinai) (1Kgs 19:10, 14) to support his point that God has not rejected his people (Rom 11:2a). Even though Elijah pleaded with God against Israel, states Paul (Rom 11:2b–4), the LORD kept for himself seven thousand people who did not bow to Baal. "So too at the present time," writes the apostle, "there is a remnant, chosen by grace" (Rom 11:5). According to Paul, as at the time of Elijah, so now a small portion of Israel has received God's righteousness as pure gift.

Elijah's contemplative prayer to the LORD and God's response leads to action. Authentic prayer stops promoting its own agenda and waits in silence for the LORD's guidance. In other words, instead of telling God what he needs to do, real prayer is listening as the LORD tells people what they need to do! Elijah is changed by his solitude. Prayer happens to Elijah; he is led, guided, loved, and used by the LORD, all the while knowing what God wants him to do next. Furthermore, in solitudinous prayer Elijah recognizes that God is not finished with him; he still has a mission to complete. No one knows Elijah's new mission except God and Elijah. He, like other people, is an instrument for enacting God's will, even if it means anointing rival kings! The LORD's promise is that seven thousand people (a sacred number: three [divine] plus four [earth] times a thousand [immensity]) have kept his covenant, have not torn down his altars, and have not killed his prophets. The LORD reveals that that remnant is as faithful as Elijah has been.

**Journal/Meditation:** In which natural elements (wind, water, snow, fire, etc.) have you discovered the divine presence? Did that discovery lead you into silent contemplation? After praying did you know what you needed to do? Explain.

FROM CONTEMPLATION TO ACTION

**Prayer:** I have been zealous for you, LORD, God of hosts. Keep me faithful to your covenant, and guide me to adore you at your altars now and forever. Amen.

## ELISHA APPEARS

**Scripture:** Elijah "found Elisha son of Shaphat, who was plowing. Elijah passed by him and threw his mantle over him." (1 Kgs 19:19ac)

**Read:** 1 Kings 19:19–21

**Reflection:** After experiencing the theophany on Mount Horeb (Sinai) and receiving a three-fold mission from the LORD, Elijah leaves the mountain to find Elisha, son of Shaphat, whom he is to anoint as his successor. In other words, Elijah paradoxically sets out to enact the last part of his mission first. And so Elijah finds Elisha plowing a field with twelve yoke of oxen. Not only do the twenty-four oxen present Elisha as possessing some wealth, but the twelve yoke is meant to echo the twelve stones Elijah erected into an altar on Mount Carmel (1 Kgs 18:31–32). The point of mentioning the twelve yoke of oxen is to note the sacred number twelve (three, the divine, plus four, the earth, plus five, the books of Torah, equal twelve), the mythological number of the tribes of Israel and Judah. In other words, like Elijah, Elisha is prophet for all God's people.

Just as Elijah had appeared suddenly in the First Book of Kings (17:1), Elisha appears suddenly in the narrative (19:19). Nothing is known about him. Indeed, there is not even the name of a place where Elijah finds him. Nevertheless, as Elijah passes by Elisha, he takes off his mantle and drapes it over Elisha's shoulders. The mantle, most likely made of animal skin covered in goat or camel hair and held in place with a leather belt (2 Kgs 1:8; Zech 13:4; Matt 3:4), is a sign of Elijah's prophetic position in Israel. When he wraps Elisha in it, he is designating him as his replacement. It is equivalent to anointing him as his successor.

Once Elisha realizes what has just occurred, he tells Elijah that he needs to say goodbye to his father and mother. Elisha reminds him that he has just received an important commission, and Elisha responds by slaughtering the oxen, burning the plowing equipment in order to boil the meat, and giving the food to people to eat. Not only does Elisha provide a goodbye feast of steak, but he makes it very clear that he is leaving his former life behind in order to follow Elijah. The author of Luke's Gospel most likely has this scene from the First Book of Kings in mind when he portrays Jesus hearing someone say, "I will follow you, Lord; but let me first say farewell to those at my home," and responding, "No one who puts a hand to the plow and looks back is fit for the kingdom of God" (Luke 9:61–62). For Jesus, there is more urgency to answering the call than there is for Elisha.

Elijah's call of Elisha is a reminder that God calls people through other people, who are willing instruments of the LORD. It is out of his contemplation on Mount Horeb (Sinai) that Elijah hears God's direction to find Elisha and call him as Elijah's successor. Thus, every person is both called and commissioned to call others, all the while being aware that it is God working through his or her contemplation. The call may come through one's cell phone, the words of an article, book, or speaker, or the action of another inviting a person for coffee, ice cream, or lunch. While it is probably unlikely today, the call may come while one is plowing a field. Out of contemplation a person both recognizes the call and calls another. Such prayerful solitude leads to prophetic action.

**Journal/Meditation**: Who has called you to serve God? Whom have you called to serve God? Did the calls emerge from solitude? What was the urgency of responding to the call? What action flowed out of the contemplative call?

**Prayer**: I will follow you, LORD, wherever you send me, and I will call others to enter into your service. Make me fit for your kingdom now and forever and ever. Amen.

## NABOTH'S VINEYARD: PART 1

**Scripture**: "Naboth the Jezreelite had a vineyard in Jezreel beside the palace of King Ahab of Samaria." (1 Kgs 21:1b)

**Read**: 1 Kings 21:1b–16

**Reflection**: The sixteen verses of chapter 21 of the First Book of Kings set the stage for Elijah's re-entry before King Ahab of Israel. Naboth, a citizen of Jezreel, owns a vineyard near Ahab's palace in Jezreel; the royal palace was located in Samaria. The king wants the owner's vineyard so that he can turn it into a vegetable garden. He is willing to make a deal with Naboth, giving him a better vineyard in exchange for his or giving him its value in cash (1 Kgs 21:2). Naboth considers the vineyard his ancestral inheritance (1 Kgs 21:3), which is protected by the law of non-alienation of patrimony (Lev 25:23–24).

## From Contemplation to Action

Not having any success in getting the land, King Ahab goes home resentful and sullen. Acting like a child, the king stretches out on his bed, turns his face toward the wall, and refuses to eat. His wife, Jezebel, whose prophets Elijah had killed (1 Kgs 18:40), finds him and inquires about his depression (1 Kgs 21:4–5). Ahab explains to her what had happened to him in his dealing with Naboth. Being a powerful woman, Jezebel reminds her husband that he is King of Israel and has every right to have whatever he wants. She exhorts him to get out of bed, to eat, and to be happy because she will find a way to get Naboth's vineyard (2 Kgs 21:6–7).

Jezebel's method of acquiring the vineyard is nothing but immoral. She writes letters to the elders and nobles in Jezreel directing them to proclaim a day of fast and bring in two men who will accuse Naboth of not keeping the fast; thus, he will be stoned to death for having cursed God and king by not observing the fast. She signs Ahab's name to the letters and seals them with his royal seal. Thus, they look like they have come from the king himself. Not wanting not to obey the king, the men, elders, and nobles of Jezreel do as they thought the king had instructed. Then, they send word to Jezebel informing her that Naboth is dead (1 Kgs 21:8–14).

Once Naboth is dead his vineyard is ready to be taken by King Ahab. Jezebel informs her husband that Naboth is now out of the picture. All he needs to do is to go take possession of the vineyard which Naboth would not trade or sell. In other words, Jezebel has been victorious. So Ahab sets out to the vineyard most recently belonging to Naboth to take possession of it (1 Kgs 21:15–16).

This story is one filled with immorality. It displays greed. It shows the extent someone will go to get what she wants her husband to have. First, Jezebel writes letters in her husband's name; while this fact does not let King Ahab off the hook, it implies complicity on his part. Second, Jezebel's letters, because they carry the royal seal, draw the elders and nobles of Jezreel into her immoral circle. They do her bidding under the pretense of obeying the king's order. When Ahab hears that Naboth is dead, he takes off immediately to lay claim to the vineyard. The heap of injustice—not to mention the breaking of the law concerning stealing property—done to Naboth, including his murder, sets the stage for the re-entry of the prophet Elijah.

**Journal/Meditation**: Today, where do you see greed as the primary motivator of people's lives? Give specific examples. Where do you see the same or similar injustice that was inflicted upon Naboth by Jezebel and Ahab? Give specific examples.

**Prayer**: Gracious God, you gave land to your chosen people, but some with power stole it from them. Make me see the injustices that surround me today, and give me the strength to speak against them that your justice may prevail now and forever. Amen.

## NABOTH'S VINEYARD: PART 2

**Scripture**: "Then the word of the LORD came to Elijah the Tishbite, saying: Go down to meet King Ahab of Israel, who rules in Samaria: he is now in the vineyard of Naboth, where he has gone to take possession." (1 Kgs 21:17–18)

**Read**: 1 Kings 21:17–29

**Reflection**: After he has anointed Elisha as his successor, Elijah disappears from the story for a while almost as suddenly as he had appeared! Out of his solitude, he hears the word of the LORD sending him to the king and queen who hate him: Ahab and Jezebel. But out of his contemplation Elijah is ready again to announce the LORD's harsh words and to take action. The first thing Elijah says to Ahab when he finds him in Naboth's vineyard is a curse about the dogs licking Ahab's blood in the same place where they licked Naboth's blood. This prophetic curse—a solemn, spoken utterance which is endowed with a certain reality which enables it to pursue its object inexorably—tells Ahab that what was done to Naboth by Jezebel (and Ahab) will be done to Ahab (and Jezebel). Elijah's confrontation of Ahab resembles Moses' confrontation of pharaoh (Exod 5:1–2; 6:10; 7:1–2, etc.). Ahab's response to Elijah is to call him his enemy because the supposedly hidden information about how Ahab has come to possess Naboth's vineyard is being revealed by Elijah.

Elijah wastes no time explaining what is going to take place because Ahab has sold himself to doing evil in the sight of the LORD. God is going to bring Ahab's (the Omride) dynasty to an end, like he did two previous times to kings (Jeroboam and Baasha) of Israel (1 Kgs 14:7–14; 16:1–4). Furthermore, because Jezebel set in motion the plot that resulted in Naboth's death, Elijah declares that her body will be eaten by dogs in Jezreel.

At this point in the story, the narrator gets carried away with a personal note. He editorializes that Ahab stands out as the king who did the most evil in the LORD's sight, urged to do so by his wife Jezebel. According to the narrator's two verses, Ahab's idolatry was most abominable (1 Kgs 21:25–26).

After hearing Elijah's words about his Omride dynasty coming to an end, Ahab tears his clothes, puts on sackcloth, fasts, and goes about with his head bent down. In other words, the king repents—as least outwardly. The word of the LORD coming to Elijah states that he also repents inwardly. At a time of crisis, seeing his own end, knowing that God has come near, Ahab enacts repentance. Thus, Elijah receives the news from the LORD that Ahab's dynasty will not end with his death, but it will come to an end with the reign of his descendents. The efficaciousness of Elijah's curse of the Omride dynasty to which Ahab belongs is transferred to his son, Ahaziah, who walked in the footsteps of his father, fell through a window lattice, and died after reigning about two years. Because he had no son, Ahaziah's brother, Jehoram (Joram), succeeded to the throne for seven years but was assassinated by Jehu, an army general, who was anointed King of Israel at Elisha's direction in fulfillment of the LORD's words to Elijah (1 Kgs 19:16). While the LORD showed mercy to Ahab because of his repentance, the Omride dynasty came to an end nevertheless.

However, Elijah's words about the dogs licking Ahab's blood where they licked Naboth's blood is fulfilled (1 Kgs 21:19:b). In a battle with the Arameans, Ahab is struck by an arrow and, after bleeding all over his chariot, he dies (1 Kgs 22:34–35). The blood is washed out of the chariot by the pool of Samaria, where the dogs lick the blood (1 Kgs 22:38). Also, Elijah's words about Jezebel's body eaten by dogs is fulfilled after eunuchs throw her out of a window of the palace in Jezreel and horses trample her body (2 Kgs 9:30–37). The rest of Ahab's family, his seventy sons and any others—leaders, close friends, and priests—who were left of his house in Jezreel are killed by Jehu either indirectly or directly concerning the word of the LORD spoken by Elijah (2 Kgs 10:1–11).

The conclusion of the story about Naboth's vineyard and the conclusion of the Omride dynasty demonstrate spirituality—a way of life—that is out of balance. King Ahab's imbalance is demonstrated by his childish behavior when Naboth refuses to sell him his vineyard and, after Naboth is stoned, by his arrogant, unjust attempt to take possession of the land. Queen Jezebel's imbalance is seen in her elaborate plot to have Naboth killed and in her arrogant, unjust giving of Naboth's vineyard to her husband. The result of all imbalances is death.

Ahab's and Jezebel's imbalances are contrasted to Elijah's balance between contemplation and action. Indeed, Elijah's life is one of an endless pursuit of both personal balance and balance for the Kingdom of Israel in terms of her king and queen. Repeatedly, Elijah demonstrates how action flows out of solitary contemplation, which, in turn, leads back to action. He appears on the scene only when he needs to be present to announce the LORD's words to those who are out of balance. Paradoxically, Elijah saves his life and the lives of many in Israel by being willing to lose it when confronting royalty at God's direction. The drought and the stealing of Naboth's vineyard reflect the lack of justice by the royal rulers. Ahab and Jezebel represent spiritual drought. Together, with no contemplation, they act only in their own self-interest.

**Journal/Meditation**: In your life, how do you practice contemplation that leads to action and back to contemplation? When you experience spiritual dryness, do you also experience death? Explain. Where do you find abominable evil in the world today? Is your spirituality in balance or out of balance? Explain how you know.

**Prayer**: O LORD, because of the evil Ahab and Jezebel brought to Israel, you brought disaster on the royal house. Make me aware of my evil that I may repent, humble myself before you, and receive your mercy now and forever. Amen.

## AHAZIAH'S DEATH

**Scripture**: "Ahaziah had fallen through the lattice in his upper chamber in Samaria, and lay injured; so he sent messengers, telling them, 'Go, inquire of Baal-zebub, the god of Ekron, whether I shall recover from this injury.'" (2 Kgs 1:2)

**Read**: 2 Kings 1:2–17

**Reflection**: As indicated in the previous entry, after Ahab's death his son, Ahaziah (853–852 BCE), succeeds him to the throne, reigning for about two years and serving Baal as his father had done (1 Kgs 22:51). The king fell through the lattice of an upper chamber window in the palace in Samaria. A lattice is an interwoven open-mesh frame made by crisscrossing strips of wood or metal to cover a window; it admits light and air while providing privacy, but it is not strong enough to keep someone, like Ahaziah, from falling through the window. Ahaziah has severely injured himself and lies on his bed wondering if he is going to die or not.

He decides to send messengers to a local representation of Baal, Baal-zebub—meaning *lord of the fly* and a mocking biblical distortion of Baal-zebul, meaning *Baal the prince*—to divine his future, that is, to find out if he will recover from his injury. As the messengers are on their way, the angel of the LORD tells Elijah to leave his solitude and to meet the king's messengers, asking them if there is no God in Israel that they could consult. Furthermore, the angel tells Elijah what to say to King Ahaziah: "You shall not leave the bed to which you have gone, but you shall surely die" (2 Kgs 1:4). After getting his instructions, Elijah sets off to meet the messengers.

There is no indication in the story that he meets them, but the next verse indicates that the meeting has taken place because they have returned to the king with the same words the angel spoke to Elijah. However, the messengers have no idea whom they met until the king asks them: "'What sort of man was he who came to meet you and told you these things?' They answered him, 'A hairy man, with a leather belt around his waist.' He said, 'It is Elijah the Tishbite'" (2 Kgs 1:7–8). Thus, Ahaziah has determined that he will be confronted by Elijah, the man wearing the hairy mantle and a leather belt, for his idolatry, just as his father, Ahab, was.

Ahaziah decides to seek the answer to his question about surviving his injury by sending a military captain with fifty men to bring Elijah to his sick bed. The captain finds Elijah sitting on the top of a hill. He addresses him as a man of God whom the king wants to see. The fifty men (five, meaning grace, multiplied by ten, meaning totality) and their captain are consumed immediately by God's fire from heaven when the man of God requests it. Fifty men and their captain are no match for the man of God! The heavenly, consuming fire—lightning—is meant to echo the fire of the LORD that fell and consumed the offering, wood, stones, dust, and water on Mount Carmel (1 Kgs 18:38). The captain and his fifty men represent the evil Ahaziah, and that is the reason they are destroyed by God's fire. Furthermore, their destruction at the divine and powerful word of Elijah prefigures Ahaziah's imminent death.

A second time this same scenario is repeated. And it looks like it is about to be repeated a third time to indicate the divine presence, but the captain pleads with Elijah to look upon his life and the lives of his fifty men as precious in light of what has already happened to two captains and one hundred men. The angel of the LORD reappears to Elijah and tells him to do what King Ahaziah requests and go with the captain. The angel guarantees Elijah's safety, so Elijah obeys and goes. When he gets to Ahaziah's bedside, he tells him that because he sent messengers to Baal to divine his future, thinking that there was no God in Israel, he will not leave his bed; he will die in it.

And so it happens. Ahaziah dies according to the word of the LORD spoken by Elijah. Because Ahaziah has no son, his brother, Jehoram (often presented biblically as Joram, 852–843 BCE), another of Ahab's sons (2 Kgs 3:1), succeeds him to his throne. This Jehoram (Joram) of Israel is not to be confused with King Jehoram of Judah (849–843), who was husband of Athaliah, daughter of Ahab and Jezebel (2 Chr 21:6). The writer of the Second Book of Kings states that Jehoram of Judah did evil in the sight of the LORD because he was married to Ahab's and Jezebel's daughter (2 Kgs 8:16–18). The chronicler records a letter sent to him by Elijah:

> Thus says the LORD, the God of your father David: Because you have not walked in the ways of your father Jehoshaphat or in the ways of King Asa of Judah, but have walked in the way of the kings of Israel, and have led Judah and the inhabitants of Jerusalem into unfaithfulness, as the house of Ahab led Israel into unfaithfulness, and because you also have killed your brothers, members of your father's house, who were better than yourself, see, the LORD will bring a great plague on your people, your children, your wives, and all your possessions, and you yourself will have a sever sickness with a disease of your bowels, until your bowels come out, day after day, because of the disease. (2 Chr 21:12b–15)

How is that for a curse?! Elijah's letter condemns thirty-two-year-old King Jehoram of Judah for his unfaithfulness to the covenant, for promoting idolatry, and for killing his six brothers (2 Chr 21:2, 4, 11). When he was thirty-eight years old, as Elijah had written in his letter, the LORD struck Jehoram of Judah in his bowels with an incurable disease which lasted for two years and caused him to die in agony at the age of forty (2 Chr 21:18–20).

Both King Jehoram (Joram) of Israel and King Jehoram of Judah are guilty of idolatry, whose source in both cases is Ahab and Jezebel. Jehoram (Joram) of Israel's idolatry is divination; he wants to know his future, which Elijah, a man of God, ultimately tells him. Jehoram of Judah's idolatry is unfaithfulness to the covenant; he is a murderer on David's throne. Both kings are confronted by the prophet Elijah. King Jehoram (Joram) of Israel is told face-to-face that his injury is the cause of his imminent death. King Jehoram of Judah is told by letter that his unfaithfulness is the cause of his incurable disease that leads to an agonizing death. In both cases, Elijah, a man of God, speaks or writes the efficacious words of the LORD.

Even today there is plenty of idolatry around. Many people around the world attempt to divine their future using Ouija boards, daily horoscopes, fortunetellers, palm-readers, wizards, crystals, necromancers, astrology, psychology, theosophy, etc. No matter if the words are spoken or written in articles and books, they represent attempts to know one's future without consulting God. Elijah represents trust only in the LORD; only he can divine the future. Only God can guarantee any future.

**Journal/Meditation**: In what ways have you attempted to know your future? What were the results? What is the attraction you (and others) have to wanting to know the future? Who speaks or writes words to tell you to trust God's will for you? Why is it so hard to trust God?

**Prayer**: God of Israel and Judah, grace me with trust in your future for me. When the day comes that I cannot leave my bed and am preparing for death, strengthen my faith in you alone. You are the LORD forever and ever. Amen.

## PREPARATION TO LEAVE

**Scripture**: "The company of prophets who were in Bethel came out to Elisha, and said to him, 'Do you know that today the LORD will take your master away from you?' And he said, 'Yes, I know; keep silent.'" (2 Kgs 2:3)

**Read**: 2 Kings 2:1–8

**Reflection**: The first eight verses of chapter 2 of the Second Book of Kings concerns the preparation for Elijah's translation into heaven. True to biblical form, it begins with a journey in Gilgal, a small town probably located in the Jordan valley near Jericho. There is no doubt that Elijah is leaving both Gilgal and the earth. The narrator of the story begins by stating that the LORD is about to take Elijah to heaven by a whirlwind, a column of air rotating rapidly around a core of low pressure. The whirlwind is a traditional biblical setting for a theophany (Job 38:1, 40:6; Ps 77:18; Isa 29:6, 66:15; Jer 4:13; Nah 1:3).

The journey Elijah begins involves his appointed successor, Elisha, who accompanies him on the trip. As they are getting ready to leave Gilgal, Elijah tells Elisha to remain in Gilgal as he is going on to Bethel. However, Elisha refuses to stay behind and travels with Elijah to Bethel. There, Elisha listens to the company of prophets—a group of men organized for

# Elijah

(frenetic) worship—tell him that the LORD is going to take Elijah away. He tells them to keep silent.

Once they arrive in Bethel, Elijah tells Elisha that the LORD has sent him to Jericho, and Elisha should remain in Bethel. As in the first instance, Elisha follows Elijah to Jericho, where the company of prophets there delivers the same message to Elisha as did those in Bethel. Elisha tells them to be silent.

As is true in many biblical stories, to indicate the divine presence, there is a third indicator by Elijah that the LORD has sent him to the Jordan River, and Elisha should remain in Jericho. But, as in the previous two stages of the journey, Elisha continues with Elijah to Jericho. Fifty men of the company of prophets arrive at the Jordan to witness the next set of events transpire.

The first stage of the journey of Elijah and Elisha begins in Gilgal, meaning *circle* of stones. It was the sacred place where Joshua erected twelve commemorative stones (Josh 4:19–24) after the Israelites crossed the parted waters of the Jordan, just like they had crossed the parted waters of the Sea of Reeds (Exod 14:21–22). The second stage of the journey begins at Bethel, meaning *house of God*. While Abraham spent some time in Bethel, its primary association is with Jacob (Israel), who experienced a theophany there and erected a standing memorial stone (Gen 28:10–22). The third stage of the journey begins at Jericho, where another theophany occurred after the Israelites had marched around the city for seven days: the walls fell down (Josh 6:1–21). Thus, all three (divine presence) places are sites of theophanies, appearances of the LORD. Furthermore, the journey itself is meant to remind the reader of the Israelites' pilgrimage for forty years. Elijah's takes place in one day and prepares for the theophany that is about to occur in a whirlwind.

At the final stop of the journey, the Jordan River, Elijah rolls up his mantle, strikes the flowing water, and watches it part so that he and Elisha can cross over on dry ground. Certainly, Elijah is patterned after Moses, who stretches out his hand over the Sea of Reeds and watches as the LORD turns it into dry land (Exod 14:21), an event repeated by Joshua at the Jordan when the priests carrying the ark of the covenant stepped into its waters and it parted so the people could cross over on dry ground (Josh 3:14–17). Elijah's mantle is equivalent to Moses' staff and the feet of the ark-bearing priests! It represents the wielding of the LORD's power. Elijah used it to appoint Elisha his successor by draping it over his shoulders (1 Kgs

19:19). The mantle represents spiritual power to act that flows out of Elijah's contemplation of God. Every time Elijah tells Elisha that he is moving on to the next place, he states that the LORD sends him to the next place (2 Kgs 2:2a, 4a, 6a). Elisha affirms this spiritual contemplative power—stating that the LORD lives and Elijah lives (2 Kgs 2:2b, 4b, 6b)—when he tells Elijah that he is going to continue to accompany him on the journey.

By reading the narrative describing the journey as the preparation for Elijah's departure, the reader suddenly discovers that journey is a double entendre. There are two meanings for the journey. The first, obviously, is going from Gilgal to Bethel, to Jericho, to the Jordan River. However, that physical journey mirrors the spiritual journey of contemplative solitude and divine activity that Elijah has been living. The last stage of the journey will be his theophanic translation into heaven in a fiery whirlwind.

It is helpful to trace the places—cities, areas, states, countries, etc.—that mark a person's journey. One can also trace it through the stages of his or her schooling, jobs, career, etc. Examining closely where one has traveled can be a contemplative experience that reveals the next steps that need to be taken. Such solitary contemplation can also reveal the divine presence which may have been overlooked during the stages of the journey.

**Journal/Meditation**: How do you prepare for your spiritual journeys? What are the five major stages of your lifetime journey? In what way was God revealed to you in each stage? How has your community (family, church, work, etc.) supported you during your journey? Why is it true to say that the LORD accompanies you on your journey to God?

**Prayer**: As you live, O LORD, and as I, myself, live, I will not take leave of my journey until I have finished the work you have entrusted to me. Through your Spirit, guide me from contemplation to action and from action to contemplation now and forever. Amen.

## ELIJAH'S DISAPPEARANCE

**Scripture**: "As [Elijah and Elisha] continued walking and talking, a chariot of fire and horses of fire separated the two of them, and Elijah ascended in a whirlwind into heaven." (2 Kgs 2:11)

**Read**: 2 Kings 2:9–12

**Reflection**: After having re-enacted the exodus crossing of the Sea of Reeds and the crossing of the Jordan into the Promised Land, Elijah asks Elisha what he can do for him before he disappears. Elisha requests a double portion of Elijah's spirit. This does not mean he asks for double the amount. Elisha is assuming the position of the first-born son, who gets a double portion of his father's inheritance. Thus, if there are three sons, the inheritance is divided into four parts, and the firstborn son gets two of those parts (Deut 21:17). In the case of two sons, the firstborn son gets two-thirds of his father's inheritance. So, Elisha asks Elijah to give him his spirit. Elijah tells Elisha that if he witnesses Elijah's disappearance, his request will be granted.

As soon as Elijah has spoken, the theophany occurs. A chariot of fire pulled by horses of fire—the LORD—descends from the heavens, picks up Elijah, and all ascend to the heavens in a whirlwind. In the Hebrew Bible (Old Testament) Book of Job, God answers Job out of the whirlwind (Job 38:1). Elisha witnesses Elijah's theophany, identifying the chariot as one of those of Israel with its horsemen. There is also an allusion here to the LORD serving as the commander of heavenly armies as Yahweh Sabaoth, meaning *the LORD of hosts* (2 Kgs 6:17). In his death-bed soliloquy, the priest Mattathias, in the First Book of Maccabees, tells those surrounding him to remember the deeds of their ancestors. Among those of previous generations, he names Elijah, who "because of great zeal for the law, was taken up into heaven" (1 Macc 2:58). As soon as Elijah disappears from his sight, Elisha tears his clothes into two pieces as a sign that he has witnessed a theophany and is mourning the passing of his father, mentor, and prophetic ancestor: Elijah.

The only other biblical person to be taken by God into heaven is Enoch, who walked with God until he was no more (Gen 5:24), suggesting that he did not die a normal death. While there is no biblical narrative about Moses being taken by God into heaven, he dies on Mount Nebo (Deut 34:1, 5). Because no one knows where he is buried (Deut 34:6), because the LORD knew him face to face (Deut 34:10), and because he was unequaled for all the signs and wonders that the LORD sent him to perform (Deut 34:11)—not to mention the terrifying displays of power that he performed (Deut 34:12)—it is easy to conclude that, like Enoch, he did not die a normal death. The Hebrew Bible (Old Testament) Book of Deuteronomy states that Moses died at the LORD's command and he was buried, "but no one knows his burial place" (Deut 34:6). In other words, somehow or someway Moses was taken by God into heaven.

Enoch's disappearance, Elijah's disappearance, and Moses' seeming disappearance into heaven are uniquely applied to Jesus by the author of

Luke's Gospel and the Acts of the Apostles. On the evening of resurrection, Jesus leads his disciples to Bethany, according to Luke's Gospel, where he lifts up his hands and withdraws from them, being carried up into heaven (Luke 24:50–51). In the Acts of the Apostles, written by the same author, this scene takes place forty sacred days after Jesus' resurrection. After instructing his disciples to wait for the coming of the Holy Spirit, Jesus is lifted up and a cloud takes him out of their sight (Acts 1:9). There is no doubt that the author understands this scene to be a theophany, like that of Elijah and Enoch. Jesus' lifted up hands echo Moses' lifted up hands (Exod 14:21), and the cloud, an element of most theophanies, recalls the theophany on Mount Horeb (Sinai) (Exod 19:9, 16; 24:15–18).

The cloud, Moses, and Elijah appear in the Christian Bible (New Testament) narration of Jesus' transfiguration, another way to name a theophany. This is especially important to the author of Luke's Gospel, who writes about Moses and Elijah appearing in glory and speaking to Jesus about his departure (exodus) (Luke 9:31), that is, his ascension, as noted above, when a cloud comes and overshadows them (Luke 9:34). Of course, the theophanic character of this narrative is enhanced with other elements of biblical theophanies; it takes place on a mountain (Luke 9:28), the typical place for theophanies to occur, eight days (completeness) after some of Jesus' teaching (Luke 9:28); three apostles—Peter, James, John—accompany Jesus (Luke 9:28); the glory of three men—Moses, Elijah, Jesus—is revealed (Luke 9:29, 31); Peter wants to build three dwellings (Luke 9:33); and a voice comes from the cloud identifying Jesus as God's chosen son (Luke 9:35).

Luke found this story in Mark's Gospel where it occurs six incomplete days after some of Jesus' teaching (Mark 9:2) on a high mountain (Mark 9:2). It is clear that the three sets of three that are found in Luke came from Mark (9:2, 4, 5), although Elijah is named before Moses in the second set of three men (Mark 9:4), clearly indicating the source of Mark's story being the translation of Elijah (and Moses) into heaven. Furthermore, the voice from the cloud identifies Jesus as God's son, the beloved, to whom Peter, James, and John should listen (Mark 9:8). Mark wrote this story to show Jesus' glorification (resurrection) after his death, since the author provides no post-resurrection appearances of Christ at the original ending of Mark 16:8. Two more endings were added at a later date to Mark's Gospel in order to supply what other authors determined was missing (Mark 16:9–20). Following in the footsteps of Greek tragedy, the author of Mark's Gospel ends his account of the good news (Mark 1:1) with the death and burial of Jesus (Mark 15:33–47). Three divine, spice-bearing women go to his tomb after the sabbath and find the stone covering the entrance rolled away and a young man, who proclaims that Jesus has been raised. The young man tells the women to go announce this to Jesus' disciples, but they leave in fear and say nothing to anyone (Mark 16:4–8). Because of the original ending of the gospel, Mark's account of the transfiguration serves as a post-resurrection appearance of Jesus before he is crucified, dead, and buried!

The author of Matthew's Gospel, like the author of Luke's Gospel, rewrites the story he finds in Mark's Gospel. Because Matthew's Gospel has two post-resurrection appearances of Christ (Matt 28:9–10; 16–20), the account of the transfiguration is presented as a metamorphosis. Jesus shines like the sun (Matt 17:2) when Moses and Elijah appear talking with him (Matt 17:3). While Matthew considers this an as-yet-incomplete resurrection foreshadowing, occurring six days after some of Jesus' teaching (Matt 17:1), he keeps all the other elements of a theophany he found in Mark's Gospel: three disciples—Peter, James, John (Matt 17:1); three men in glory—Moses, Elijah, Jesus (Matt 17:2–3); three dwellings (Matt 17:4); a bright overshadowing cloud (Matt 17:5); and a voice that instructs the disciples to listen to Jesus, God's beloved son with whom he is pleased (Matt 17:5). Up to this point in his account, Matthew has been presenting Jesus as a new Moses (Matt 2:7–23) and John the Baptist as a new Elijah (Matt 3:4; 17:10–13) about which more will be written below.

Elijah's translation into heaven removes him from the visible world to the invisible one. The whirlwind serves as the portal between the two. In the Bible's three-storied universe, the whirlwind forms the portal that connects the world below, where people live, to the world above, where the LORD lives. When they come together, like they did for Elijah, the result is human wholeness and divine holiness converging in one person. In other words, Elijah was the fiery whirlwind, uniting in himself the human and the divine. The divine Spirit was a work in the human matter, Elijah's body. While the divine Spirit, the LORD, could not be seen, it could be contemplated in solitude where it opened the prophet on earth to see the universal. The concrete circumstances of time (eighth century BC) and place (Israel) open to the big picture of God's world which even Elijah could not fully see. God's fire, the divine presence, was incarnate in Elijah, who, through solitary contemplation and fiery signs, became aware of it. What Jesus says of John the Baptist in John's Gospel is applicable to Elijah: "He was a burning and shining lamp . . ." (John 5:35). Elijah, Israel's guide and source of security, was translated into heaven and transfigured into glory. His sudden disappearance matches his sudden appearance (1 Kgs 17:1)!

**Journal/Meditation**: What have been some of the transfiguring experiences of your life? In what specific ways did you experience the divine Spirit at work? What portal connected your visible world to the invisible one? What signs of the glory of the divine were present?

**Prayer**: O LORD, because of his great zeal for your law, you took Elijah into heaven. Continue to transfigure me with your divine Spirit that your fiery chariot and fiery horses may take me to heaven after a life in your service. Amen.

## ELIJAH'S POWER

**Scripture**: "[Elisha] took the mantle of Elijah that had fallen from him, and struck the water [of the Jordan River], saying, 'Where is the LORD, the God of Elijah?' When he had struck the water, the water was parted to the one side and to the other, and Elisha went over." (2 Kgs 2:14)

**Read**: 2 Kings 2:13–18

**Reflection**: After Elijah's disappearance, Elisha notices that Elijah's powerful mantle had fallen from him. So, he picks it up and walks back to the Jordan River. Knowing that the mantle represents and somehow contains the LORD's power at work in Elijah, Elisha wants to know if it has been transferred to him as Elijah's successor. After rolling up the mantle he asks the LORD if God's power now exists in himself. Then, he gets an answer as he strikes the water in the Jordan River and it parts for him to cross over on dry land, just as it had done for Elijah, Joshua before, and just as the Sea of Reeds had parted for Moses before that. This transfer of power from Elijah to Elisha is like the transfer of power from Moses to Joshua (Num 27:18–23; Deut 34:9).

The company of prophets who had waited for Elisha at Jericho (2 Kgs 2:7) see him approaching and declare, "The spirit of Elijah rests on Elisha" (2 Kgs 2:15). In other words, Elisha's request for a double portion of Elijah's spirit has been granted (2 Kgs 2:9), as was demonstrated when Elisha parted the waters of the Jordan River. When Elisha gets close to the company of prophets, the fifty of them bow before him in recognition of his new status as a man of God and petition him to let them go and, hopefully, find Elijah. Because Elijah has a tendency to disappear after having been caught up in the LORD's spirit, as narrated by Obadiah (1 Kgs 18:11–12), the prophets suggest that this may have happened again and Elijah can be found either on a mountain or in a valley. At first Elisha tells them not to go, but, after they persist, he lets the fifty men search for three days (divine presence) without finding him. Elisha knows they cannot find Elijah because he has been taken to heaven.

While the fifty prophets are out scouring the area for Elijah, Elisha remains at Jericho in solitude. For this man of God, it is "a time to keep silence" (Eccl 3:7b), to let gentle silence envelope all things (Wis 18:14a). In the midst of dead calm (Mark 4:39; Matt 8:26), Elisha prepares himself through contemplation for the activity in which he will be engaged as prophetic leader of Israel. That activity flowing out of contemplation will be explored in chapter 2 of this book.

Elijah's translation into heaven led the post-exilic prophet Malachi to declare a coming day of God's judgment which would be preceded by the LORD sending Elijah, who, as God's messenger, would turn the hearts of parents to their children and those of children to their parents (Mal 4:5). Malachi's unique mention of Elijah's return led Christian Bible (New Testament) writers to declare that the judgment day arrives with the preaching of John the Baptist, who is Elijah reappeared. In Mark's Gospel, when Jesus' disciples ask him about Elijah's coming (Mark 9:11), he states that Elijah must come first to restore all things (Mark 9:12a). Then, he tells them that Elijah has already come, but he does not explicitly identify John the Baptist with him (Mark 9:13). Implicitly, using the same description of John the Baptist's clothes as that used for Elijah—camel's hair with a leather belt (Mark 1:6)—John the Baptist is clearly Elijah returned.

The author of Matthew's Gospel keeps the description of John the Baptist's clothing resembling Elijah that he found in Mark's Gospel (Matt 3:4), but also portrays Jesus explicitly declaring that John is Elijah who was to come (Matt 11:14) and who has already come unrecognizably (Matt 17:10–12a). The author of Luke's Gospel is very clear that John the Baptist possesses the spirit and power of Elijah (Luke 1:17) and is Elijah reappeared (Luke 9:8). However, in John's Gospel, John the Baptist makes it clear that he is not Elijah (John 1:21bc, 25). Thus, there is ambiguity between the Synoptic Gospels (Mark, Matthew, Luke) and John's Gospel. It seems that, paradoxically, John the Baptist is Elijah returned and he is not Elijah returned!

In Mark's Gospel, immediately before Jesus dies, some of the bystanders think Jesus is calling for Elijah (Mark 15:35) and someone says to wait and see whether Elijah will come to take him down from the cross (Mark 15:36). Elijah does not appear. The same scenario is narrated by the author of Matthew's Gospel, because he is using Mark's Gospel as his source (Matt 27:47, 49). The author of Luke's Gospel does not follow his Markan source for Jesus' crucifixion; thus, he does not present the scene found in Mark's Gospel and Matthew's Gospel.

Some people think that Jesus is Elijah returned. The author of Mark's Gospel records that Herod heard reports that Jesus is Elijah (Mark 6:15), and some of Jesus' disciples tell him that some people are saying that he is Elijah (Mark 8:28). Because the author of Matthew's Gospel has clearly equated John the Baptist with Elijah (Matt 11:14), he omits all reports about Jesus being Elijah. However, he does narrate that Jesus' disciples report that some people think that he, the Son of Man, is Elijah (Matt 16:14). The author of Luke's Gospel keeps his Markan source about Herod receiving a report that Jesus is Elijah reappeared (Luke 9:8) along with his Markan source that Jesus' disciples report that crowds declare him to be Elijah (Luke 9:19).

Elijah, as has been seen, has a definite affect on Christian Bible (New Testament) writers. This is due to Elisha's request for a double portion of Elijah's spirit which is granted to him. The author of Luke's Gospel in particular endows John the Baptist with the spirit and power of Elijah, in a way modeling his reception of such on Elisha. The spirit and power of Elijah continues today through divine intervention. God connects with people in ways of which they may not even be aware. Every daily event that people experience has the potential to be a divine encounter, an opportunity to receive and use the spirit and power of Elijah, like Elisha did. Awareness of this connection comes through contemplation—immersion in gentle silence that so envelops one that he or she can hear the word of the LORD—that leads to action. It will be paradoxical; contemplation brings together construction of some of life and destruction of some of life as only God can do. That is what the spirit and power of Elijah did throughout his life. Elijah constructed a world filled with the LORD's presence, and destructed a world full of idols. Elijah's spirit and power can be passed on, as seen in its reception by Elisha.

**Journal/Meditation**: How have you experienced the spirit and power of Elijah? How is contemplative solitude a part of your experience? To what action did it lead you? Why do you think Christian Bible (New Testament) writers identify John the Baptist and Jesus with Elijah?

# Elijah

**Prayer**: Before your great and terrible day, O LORD, you promised to send the prophet Elijah to turn people's hearts to each other and to you. Let me inherit a double share of Elijah's spirit and power that will praise you now and forever. Amen.

## ELIJAH SUMMARY

**Scripture**: ". . . Elijah arose, a prophet like fire, and his word burned like a torch." (Sir 48:1)

**Read**: Sirach 48:1–11

**Reflection**: The Old Testament (Apocrypha) Book of Sirach, also known as Ecclesiasticus, contains a six-chapter section entitled "Hymn in Honor of Our Ancestors." Among those ancestors included in the hymn is Elijah, who is described as a prophet like fire! Basically, the first eleven verses of chapter 48 of Sirach summarize Elijah's deeds in the Northern Kingdom of Israel during the reigns of King Ahab (874–853 BCE), King Ahaziah (853–852 BCE), and King Jehoram (Joram) (852–843 BCE). According to Sirach, the prophet brought a famine, shutting the heavens, yet three times invoked God's heavenly fire—lightning—on Mount Carmel. He raised a corpse—the son of the widow of Zarephath—from the dead.

He declared to King Ahaziah, Ahab's son, that he would die after Ahaziah had tried to capture him three times with a military captain commanding fifty men! On Mount Horeb (Sinai) he listened to the LORD tell him about his judgment on Israel and how he was preserving seven thousand people who had remained faithful to him. Spreading his mantle over Elisha, he proclaimed him to be his successor. Then, he was taken by a whirlwind of fire in a chariot of fire pulled by horses of fire into heaven. And at the appointed time, Elijah will return to restore the tribes of Jacob (Israel).

The author of Sirach, named Jesus son of Sirach, praises Elijah as a prophet who spoke in prophetic oracles (Sir 44:3b), one who left behind a name so that others can praise him (Sir 44:8), a godly man, whose righteous deeds have not been forgotten (Sir 44:10). He gets so caught up in narrating Elijah's deeds that he declares: "How glorious you were, Elijah, in your wondrous deeds! Whose glory is equal to yours?" (Sir 48:4) And he concludes his reflections on the prophet by writing: "Happy are those who saw you [, Elijah,] and were adorned with your love! For we also shall surely live" (Sir 48:11).

A reference in the apocryphal apocalypse known as Second Esdras (Fourth Ezra) also mentions Elijah. The author presents a list of biblical persons who represent biblical precedents for prayer on behalf of sinners. In that list, he states that "Elijah [prayed] for those who received the rain, and for the one who was dead, that he might live" (2 Esd 7:39 [7:109]). The former reference to praying for rain refers to the rain that fell after the events on Mount Carmel; the latter reference refers to Elijah's raising of the widow of Zarephath's son.

Most people cannot begin to achieve the deeds credited to Elijah. However, most families possess the memory of ancestors who left a name for themselves in some way. They are remembered at family gatherings because they were righteous; they did the right thing in their time and place because it was the right thing to do. They were not prophets in the common understanding of predicting the future. Rather, they were people who contemplated the divine in solitude while driving, hiking, or sailing. They came to know God's will for them through their solitary contemplation, and, once the LORD's will was known, they enacted it through the daily activity of their lives. Indeed, they should be remembered and praised!

**Journal/Meditation**: Who are the ancestors in your family remembered at family gatherings? Make a list of their names and identify the quality or virtue for which each is held in memory? Also note how each is an example of contemplation leading to action and action leading back to contemplation.

**Prayer**: How glorious you made your prophet Elijah, O LORD, in wondrous deeds! His glory is unequaled to those who saw him, to those who experienced his love! I praise you for the words and deeds of Elijah now and forever. Amen.

# 2

# Elisha

# From Contemplation to Action

## PURIFIED SPRING

**Scripture:** "... [Elisha] went to the spring of water and threw the salt into it, and said, 'Thus says the LORD, I have made this water wholesome; from now on neither death nor miscarriage shall come from it.'" (2 Kgs 2:21)

**Read:** 2 Kings 2:19–22

**Reflection:** After witnessing his predecessor ascend to heaven in a fiery chariot with fiery horses in a whirlwind and having picked up Elijah's mantle of power and used it to part the waters of the Jordan River, Elisha, whose name means *God has saved*, is ready to wield the LORD's power as a man of God. He has spent three days in contemplation in Jericho. The citizens of Jericho approach him and report that their city has a good location, but a bad water supply leads to unfruitfulness (miscarriage). Acting on their words, Elisha instructs them to bring him a new bowl with salt in it. The new bowl indicates that it has had no profane use and serves as a fitting medium for the divine. Salt was understood to repel evil; it was offered with sacrificial victims in the temple in order to remove any (unseen) corruption that may have clung to a gift meant for the LORD (Lev 2:13; Ezek 43:24). Besides serving as a purifying agent, salt is also a preservative; it keeps the sacrifice fresh until it is consumed by fire.

After Elisha throws the salt in the spring, it becomes permanently purified and fit for human drinking. People will no longer die from drinking the bad water, and women will no longer miscarry because they drink it. Wholesomeness is the result of Elisha's action. The custom of throwing a small amount of salt over one's shoulder stems from Elisha's activity; it is meant to keep away evil from a person. If he or she is cooking, it is meant to purify the food and make it safe to eat. That is wholesomeness!

In the Christian Bible (New Testament), Jesus tells his disciples that they will be salted with fire (Mark 9:49); this is the first of three unrelated sayings that the author of Mark's Gospel has collected using the catchword salt. This first saying probably refers to salt's purifying quality, just like fire purifies metals. The second saying, identical to one found also in Luke's Gospel (14:34) poses a statement followed by a question: "Salt is good; but if salt has lost it saltiness, how can you season it?" (Mark 9:50a). This saying seems to refer to defection; if disciples leave Jesus, they cannot be restored. This interpretation is confirmed by both Matthew's and Luke's additional verse of explanation about salt no longer being good for anything and being thrown out and trampled underfoot (Matt 5:13b) or it being neither fit for the soil nor for the manure pile (Luke 14:35a). The third saying in Mark's

Gospel is unique: "Have salt in yourselves, and be at peace with one another" (Mark 9:50b); it probably refers to the charity which enables people to get along well with each other. There is also a unique verse in Matthew's Gospel in which Jesus tells his disciples that they are the salt of the earth (Matt 5:13a), indicating that they both season and purify the world with their teaching and example.

Elisha's act of purifying the spring with salt appears in *The Roman Missal*. In the "Rite for the Blessing and Sprinkling of Water," the priest or bishop has the option of blessing salt before he pours it into the blessed water. The prayer for blessing salt recalls the prophet Elisha's casting of salt into water so that the impure water could be purified. However, there is also mention in the prayer of the salt and water repulsing the attack of the enemy and God's Holy Spirit being present to keep all safe at all times.

Elisha draws no division between the common and the sacred. He uses a common bowl with common salt to bring the sacred to purify the spring. In other words, all is charged with the LORD's Spirit. That is why after pouring the salt into the water Elisha declares words from the LORD. Water is a universal portal to the divine. Moses parted the Sea of Reeds to open the portal to divine freedom. Joshua parted the Jordan River to open the portal to the Promised Land. Elijah parted the Jordan River to open the portal to the whirlwind that took him to heaven. Elisha parted the Jordan River to open the portal to his status as successor to Elijah and a man of God. And Jesus opened the portal to God's kingdom by being baptized in the Jordan River and seeing the heavens torn apart and the Spirit descending upon him (Mark 1:10). For those with spiritual eyes, the world is charged with the divine; all that is needed is a prophet, like Elisha, who can point toward the portal with such simple things as a bowl and salt. Spiritually speaking, God is in all situations, even the bad ones like polluted water. Everything becomes the occasion for the spiritual, the divine, to reveal himself. Everything becomes the occasion for an encounter with God.

**Journal/Meditation:** What is the equivalent of salt's purifying and preservative characteristics today? Have you ever become aware of God's presence when using or seeing salt? How are you the salt of the earth? What has attacked your wholesomeness, and what has restored it?

**Prayer:** O LORD, through the prophet Elisha, you made the spring of water wholesome with salt. Salt me with the fire of the Spirit so that I can recognize you in all things and praise you now and forever and ever. Amen.

## BEARS

**Scripture**: "When [Elijah] turned around and saw [the small boys], he cursed them in the name of the LORD. Then two she-bears came out of the woods and mauled forty-two of the boys." (2 Kgs 2:24)

**Read**: 2 Kings 2:23–25

**Reflection**: After Elisha purifies the spring near Jericho, he heads to Bethel. Some boys from Bethel see him passing and begin to jeer at him, saying, "Go away, baldhead!" (2 Kgs 2:23) After hearing them taunt him several times, he turns around and curses them in the name of the LORD. A curse is a solemn utterance which cannot be retracted or annulled and is effective. And so two she-bears come out of the woods immediately and maul forty-two of the boys! This legend about one of Elisha's actions demonstrates that Elisha has received Elijah's power, while also teaching that prophets are to be respected!

The Infancy Gospel of Thomas, an apocryphal work of the second century CE, presents a Jesus character modeled on Elisha in a few of its opening stories. The five-year-old boy Jesus is playing by the ford of a stream; he gathers the flowing waters into pools and makes them pure. It is not long until another boy arrives and, taking a willow branch, scatters the water in the pools. Jesus curses him to be withered like a tree, and he immediately withers. A while later, a child runs up and bangs into Jesus' shoulder; Jesus curses him, and the child falls down and dies! While these stories about Jesus are embarrassing to Christians, they present him as a character deserving respect for the divine power he wields.

The paradox presented in the legend of Elisha and carried over into the Infancy Gospel of Thomas also appears in Jesus' teaching in Matthew's Gospel. He teaches his disciples: "Love your enemies and pray for those who persecute you" (Matt 5:44). Engaging in such action that flows out of deep contemplation imitates God's love for the world. The LORD does not discriminate with sunshine—it is light for the bad and the good—nor with rain—it falls equally on the righteous and on the unrighteous (Matt 5:45). Human wholeness is achieved by being perfect as God is perfect (Matt 5:48). In Luke's Gospel, Jesus expands the teaching found in Matthew's Gospel, telling his disciples: "Love your enemies, do good to those who hate you, bless those who curse you, pray for those who abuse you" (Luke 6:27). In the depth of contemplation, the paradoxical truth emerges. Loving enemies and doing good indicate that a person's actions are like those of the Most High, who is kind to the ungrateful and the wicked (Luke 6:35).

Human wholeness, according to the Lukan Jesus, is being merciful, like God is merciful (Luke 6:36), that is, giving to others what is due them according to God's standards. The Lukan Jesus illustrates this when he prays on the cross: "Father, forgive them; for they do not know what they are doing" (Luke 23:34). Because those who put Jesus to death are ignorant of who he is, they cannot be held accountable for their actions. Only the crucified, contemplative Jesus can recognize that truth.

Elisha continues his journey, a principal biblical theme, to Mount Carmel, where Elijah called upon the LORD and demonstrated who the real God is in Israel. Then, Elisha goes to Samaria to serve as prophet in the same region—the Kingdom of Israel—in which Elijah ministered. Elisha knows that God is with him in everything he experiences; he finds God in every human experience, even his own human limitations and suffering, because he spends time in solitary contemplation. While he participates in the divine flow, he can be called names and he can be rejected; both acceptance and rejection are manifestations of the divine. As a prophet like Elijah, he bears the divine presence which should evoke the respect of others. Respect leads to more self-knowledge, authenticity, and awareness which emerge from contemplative solitude. Traveling alone, Elisha experiences the essence of life, truth, and the unity of all things. He sees the LORD everywhere, even in a curse, coming to recognize himself as a mirror image of God.

**Journal/Meditation**: What aspect of the Elisha legend shocks you? What does the legend teach you? Along your lifetime journey in what specific experiences—which may have appeared to be paradoxical—have you known the divine presence?

**Prayer**: Heavenly Father, through the teaching of Jesus, your Son, you have taught me to love my enemies and to pray for my persecutors. Grant me the grace to love others in praise and in curse and to pray for peacemakers and persecutors. You are LORD forever and ever. Amen.

## WADI POOLS

**Scripture**: ". . . [W]hile the musician was playing, the power of the LORD came on [Elisha]. And he said, 'Thus says the LORD, "I will make this wadi full of pools." For thus says the LORD, "You shall see neither wind nor rain, but the wadi shall be filled with water, so that you shall drink, you, your cattle, and your animals.'" The next day, about the time of the morning offering, suddenly water began to flow . . . ." (2 Kgs 3:15b–17, 20)

**Read**: 2 Kings 3:1–20

**Reflection**: In order to fully grasp this story, the stage must be set. In the Southern Kingdom of Judah, Jehoshaphat reigns (870–849 BCE) in Judah; in the Northern Kingdom of Israel, Jehoram (Joram) (852–843 BCE), son of Ahab, reigns in Samaria. King Mesha of Moab pays the yearly tribute of one hundred thousand lambs and the wool of one hundred thousand rams to the king of Israel. However, after King Ahab, Jehoram's (Joram) father, died, Mesha rebelled and refused to pay tribute to Jehoram (Joram), who declared war against Mesha. Jehoram (Joram) enlisted King Jehoshaphat of Judah and his army to assist him in bringing Mesha under control.

On their way to Moab, they also enlist the help of the king of Edom, through whose territory they pass on their way to Moab. After marching for seven days (the sum of three, the divine, and four, the earth, meaning completion), they find no water. Jehoram (Joram) immediately panics, thinking that the LORD is going to hand them over to Mesha of Moab. Jehoshaphat, however, asks about the presence of one of the LORD's prophets from whom he can divine God's will. Then, ironically, it is one of Jehoram's (Joram) servants who states, "Elisha son of Shaphat, who used to pour water on the hands of Elijah, is here" (2 Kgs 3:11b). Jehoshaphat declares that he knows that the LORD's word is with Elijah's former servant and successor. Then, the three kings go to see him.

Upon arrival, Elisha immediately addresses Jehoram (Joram) wanting to know why he has come when he has his father's (Ahab) and his mother's (Jezebel) prophets, worshipers of Baal and Asherah, to consult. Jehoram (Joram) expresses his conviction that it is the LORD who has brought together the three kings, who are in danger of being handed over to Moab. Elisha, employing a formula used by Elijah, declares, "As the LORD of hosts lives, whom I serve, were it not that I have regard for King Jehoshaphat of Judah, I would give you neither a look nor a glance" (2 Kgs 3:14). Because he has respect for the king of Judah, Elisha agrees to divine the LORD's will for the three kings.

In order to do this, the prophet calls for a musician, who begins to play. While the musician plays, Elisha enters into a trance, an ecstatic experience of the power of the LORD coming through him. It seems that harps, tambourines, flutes, and lyres were often used to create a prophetic frenzy during which the prophets were possessed by the spirit of the LORD and spoke on God's behalf (1 Sam 10:5–6; 1 Chr 25:3). Thus, on behalf of God, Elisha declares that pools of water will form in the wadi, the dry stream bed, for the soldiers and the animals to drink, but those pools will be caused by neither wind nor rain. Sure enough, at the time of the morning offering, dawn, the water begins to flow in the otherwise dry wadi. Furthermore, defeating Moab is but a trifle in the LORD's eyes declares the prophet. Elisha divines that the three kings will conquer all of Moab. The rest of the story (2 Kgs 3:21–27) explains how that is accomplished.

Just as Elijah is associated with fire, Elisha is associated with water. As seen above, the first thing the prophet does after Elijah is taken to heaven is part the waters of the Jordan River using Elijah's mantle. The second thing he does is purify the spring of water near Jericho. And his third deed of power is to cause pools of water to appear in a wadi with no thunderstorm of wind and rain. It is this latter work that especially connects him to Elijah, who, after declaring a drought, then declares the drought at an end with rain (1 Kgs 17:1; 18:45). In this Elisha story, the prophet ends the drought that exists in the dry streambed with pools of water.

The music used by Elisha to enter into ecstatic contemplation serves as the vehicle for getting in tune with the hidden moments of God's presence. Such awareness then enables him to become the vehicle for communicating the LORD's will and the action of pools of water. Music's being participates in God, who is Being itself. Thus, music provides a spiritual experience, a connection, to everything, especially the divine. Elisha is drawn to that which he has repeatedly discovered hidden deep within himself—the divine. He is what he seeks. Music enables him to find himself, and, in doing so, to find the LORD, who reveals his will to Elisha. Out of contemplation there comes action.

**Journal/Meditation:** What do you like and dislike about Elisha's attitude toward the king of Israel? Where do you find the same like and dislike in your life today? How do you use music to assist your contemplation (journaling, meditation)? What activity flows from this process?

**Prayer:** As you live, LORD of hosts, whom I serve, send your power upon me when I contemplate you. After coming to know your will, grant me the grace to enact it. You are God forever and ever. Amen.

## OIL

**Scripture**: "[Elisha] said [to the wife of a member of the company of prophets], 'Go outside, borrow vessels from all your neighbors, empty vessels and not just a few. Then go in, and shut the door behind you and your children, and start pouring [oil] into all these vessels; when each is full, set it aside.'" (2 Kgs 4:3–4)

**Read**: 2 Kings 4:1–7

**Reflection**: At the time of the activity of Elijah and Elisha, there existed companies of prophets organized for worship in cultic song and dance and living in community outside towns and cities. The members of such companies often served as messengers to Elisha. The wife of a prophet, who was a member of such a company, approaches Elisha and tells him that her husband, Elisha's servant, has died and left her in debt. Because she cannot pay the debt, her creditor is going to take her two children into slavery as payment, which was permitted by Israelite law (Lev 25:39–42; Deut 15:1–17). Elisha poses two questions to her about what she wants him to do for her and what she has in her house. Her answer reveals her poverty—a jar of oil—and immediately presents Elisha as a type of Elijah, who ministered to a widow in a similar way (1 Kgs 17:8–16).

Elisha instructs the widow to borrow empty vessels from her neighbors. Once she has collected them, she is to take them with her children inside her home and secretly begin pouring olive oil out of the jar into the empty vessels until all of them are full. This she does until all the vessels are full of oil and the jar of oil stops flowing. She reports to Elisha that all the vessels are full of oil. He tells her to take the oil to market, sell it, pay her debt, and then she and her children can live on what remains after that.

It is to be noted that this is the first deed of Elisha that does not involve water. Also, it will be repeated later with barley loaves and ears of grain (2 Kgs 4:42–44). The amount of olive oil is limited only by the number of empty vessels the unnamed widow can borrow. Out of a little jar of oil comes abundance. The LORD does not see scarcity when people do; the LORD sees abundance. Elisha's directions given to the woman mitigates the Torah, rendering it powerless in this situation; once she sells the oil and pays her debt her creditor cannot exercise his legal right to take her children as slaves. Furthermore, in contrast to Elijah, who spent most of his time in the wilderness disappearing and only infrequently reappearing, Elisha walks among the common people on a daily basis. He displays compassion for their poverty and enacts deeds of mercy.

Seeing abundance where many see scarcity and removing burdens remains a ministry today. Closets are often full of clothes that are no longer worn; giving those few clothes away creates abundance for the naked. Lots of food—leftover and otherwise—is thrown away; it can be abundance to the hungry if brought to a shelter. Even a book sitting on a shelf or a few old magazines in a pile can be abundant reading for one who has no access to reading material. Elisha serves as an example not only of how activity flows out of contemplation, but of how a little given away produces abundantly.

**Journal/Meditation:** What jars of oil do you have in your house that could be multiplied through giving away? What limits your giving away?

**Prayer**: LORD, the widow's jar of oil flowed until every empty vessel was full. Fill me with your grace that I may overflow into all the empty vessels I encounter this day and praise you for your abundance in the midst of scarcity forever and ever. Amen.

## SHUNAMMITE COUPLE

**Scripture**: "One day Elisha was passing through Shunem, where a wealthy woman lived, who urged him to have a meal. So whenever he passed that way, he would stop there for a meal." (2 Kgs 4:8)

**Read**: 2 Kings 4:8–17

**Reflection**: What begins as simple hospitality—an invitation to a meal—quickly turns into elaborate hospitality—a new, completely-furnished room—by a wealthy woman and her husband in Shunem, a town in the Northern Kingdom of Israel, not too far from Mount Carmel. Elisha is passing through the town, as he frequently does, and the wealthy woman, who recognizes him as a holy man of God, invites him to have a meal. Stopping in her home for a meal then becomes a regular occurrence.

After consulting with her husband, they agree to build a small room on the roof of their home and furnish it with a bed, a table, a chair, and a lamp for Elisha's comfort. The roof chamber was accessed by an outer stairway independent of the main house, much like an apartment is accessed today. According to the narrative, it seems that Elisha uses the room on a regular basis, bringing his servant, Gehazi, with him. One day Elisha instructs Gehazi to call the woman and ask her what she may need in order to thank her for providing the room. She replies that she needs nothing. Afterward, Gehazi tells Elisha that she has no son and that her elderly husband may not be able much longer to try to impregnate her. At this suggestion, Elisha calls the woman and tells her that in due season she will conceive a son. She, like other women of the past—Sarai (Gen 16:1–2) and Hannah (1 Sam 1:1–8)—considers her barrenness her greatest misfortune. In the midst of such misfortune life quickens and sons are born (Gen 21:1–2; 1 Sam 1:20). The Shunammite woman conceives and bears a son as Elisha declares.

Not only does this narrative echo that of Elijah and the widow of Zarephath (1 Kgs 17:8–16), portraying Elisha as a carbon copy of Elijah, but it also illustrates the biblical theme of showing hospitality which results in an experience of the divine. The unnamed, barren woman of Shunem is modeled on Sarah, the barren wife of Abraham. After showing hospitality to three strangers in the heat of the day (Gen 18:1), one of them tells Abraham that in due season Sarah will conceive and bear a son (Gen 18:10a). Elisha, a man of God, is modeled on Abraham's unnamed visitor, who, later in the narrative, is identified as the LORD (Gen 18:20, 22), and as an angel (Gen 19:1), the LORD in disguise. In the Christian Bible (New Testament), the author of the Letter to the Hebrews exhorts his readers not to neglect to show hospitality to strangers, because by doing so some have entertained angels without knowing it (Heb 13:2).

The showing of hospitality to Elisha by the Shunammite couple presents an example of activity leading to contemplation. After sharing meals with Elisha, the couple builds him an outside-accessible room on the roof of their house, and the prophet responds by leading them into contemplating a son. Working in a food bank can lead one to contemplate hunger. Working in a homeless shelter can lead one into deep contemplation of housing for the poor. Even the activity of teaching can lead a professor to contemplate the state of education today. In any such experiences, contemplation reveals the divine. Elisha was the recipient of the Shunammite couple's hospitality which resulted in the hidden quickening of a son at the word of the man of God.

**Journal/Meditation:** To whom have you shown hospitality only to discover that your activity led you to deeper contemplation? Who has shown you hospitality that led you to deeper contemplation? What new life stirred within you? How did you experience the divine?

**Prayer**: Grant, O LORD, that I may both worthily receive and give hospitality to all I meet and recognize your presence in the new life such encounters bring. Out of my barren contemplation bring forth divine activity now and forever. Amen.

ELISHA

## RESUSCITATION

**Scripture**: "... [Elisha] went in [to the rooftop room] and closed the door on the [woman's dead son and him], and prayed to the LORD. Then he got up on the bed and lay upon the child, putting his mouth upon his mouth, his eyes upon his eyes, and his hands upon his hands; and while he lay bent over him, the flesh of the child became warm." (2 Kgs 4:33–34)

**Read**: 2 Kings 4:18–37

**Reflection**: A number of years have passed since the birth of the son to the Shunammite couple. He is old enough to accompany his father to the fields with the reapers. One morning while with his unnamed father, the unnamed son complains about his head hurting. His father instructs his servant to take the boy home to his mother. She receives him and sits with him on her lap until noon, when he dies. Taking the boy's dead body to the roof chamber where Elisha often stays, she lays it on the man of God's bed, closes the door, and leaves. She tells her husband to send one of their servants with a donkey so that she can go get the prophet. Her husband reminds her that since it is neither new moon nor sabbath that Elisha may not be home near Mount Carmel, about a twenty-five mile trip from Shunem. Confidently, she tells him that all will be well.

She saddles the donkey, mounts, and begins her trip to Mount Carmel in the hope of getting there and getting back to Shunem the same day. She tells the animal to move as fast as possible. As she nears Mount Carmel, Elisha sees her coming and sends his servant, Gehazi, to run and meet her and ask about her, her husband, and her child. After listening to his questions, she assures Gehazi that all is well, repeating what she had told her husband before she left.

When she gets to Elisha, she embraces his feet in petition. When Gehazi attempts to push her away, Elisha tells him that she is distressed, but the LORD has not revealed to him the cause. She tells Elisha that she did not ask for a son. In fact, she asked Elisha not to mislead her by promising one to her. This information prompts Elisha to instruct Gehazi to go directly to the woman's home, taking his staff to the boy and laying it on his face. Like the staff of power that Moses wields (Exod 14:16), Elisha's staff possesses divine power. However, the woman, using prophetic language declaring the LORD living and Elisha living, states that she is not leaving without Elisha. So, he says he will follow her.

Gehazi, who left immediately with Elisha's staff, arrives at the Shunammite couple's home, enters the rooftop room, and lays the staff on the face of the child, but nothing happens. He backtracks to meet Elisha and the woman on their way, telling them that the child did not awaken. Without Elisha to wield the staff's power, the LORD will not work any wonder; Elisha is the man of God, not Gehazi. Finally, Elisha and the woman arrive, and Elisha sees the child lying dead on his bed. He closes the door on the two of them and prays to the LORD. Then, he stretches himself out on top of the child with his mouth to the child's mouth, with his eyes to the child's eyes, and with his hands to the child's hands. In other words, Elisha gives himself totally to the boy to restore his breath, his sight, and his touch—his life. This is done in silence, like that experienced by Elijah on Mount Horeb (Sinai) (1 Kgs 19:12); it is also a moment of contemplation. Elisha feels the child's body warm under his own, and he removes himself from the boy. The LORD has heard his prayer. The child has been raised from the dead!

While Elisha takes a few seconds to contemplate what the LORD has just accomplished through him, the child sneezes seven times and opens his eyes. The sneezing not only indicates that he is alive, but that he is expelling whatever demon caused his death. The seven-fold sneeze indicates that the divine (three) and the earth (four), equaling seven, have merged perfectly in the person of Elisha. The LORD (three) has touched the boy on the earth (four) using Elisha as a medium of his power. Following protocol, Elisha tells Gehazi to summon the woman, who, after arriving in the room, kneels at Elisha's feet and bows all the way to the floor, receives back her son alive and leaves.

This account of Elisha raising the dead son of the Shunammite couple becomes the model for the account of Jesus raising a dead girl in the Christian Bible (New Testament). The author of Mark's Gospel records a story about a synagogue leader named Jairus, whose daughter is dead. Jesus goes to Jairus's home, enters the room where the dead child lay, and declares that the twelve-year-old girl is sleeping. He takes her by the hand, says a magical incantation in Aramaic, and watches as she gets up (Mark 5:21–24, 35–43). The same story is found in a shortened version in Matthew's Gospel (9:18–19, 23–26) and in Luke's Gospel (8:41–42, 49–56).

Elisha is a conduit for divine power. The story's narrative moves from action (going to Shunem) to contemplation (silently praying and stretching himself over the boy) to action (returning the child to his mother). The wealthy woman of Shunem is a believer in the LORD and in his prophet, the man of God. She indicates this by inviting him to dine with her and her husband, by building a rooftop room for him, and by declaring that all will be well. She trusts that the LORD can use his man of God, Elisha, to restore her son to life. She, a woman, has faith that the LORD has everything under control.

**Journal/Meditation:** How is your faith like that woman of Shunem? In what experience of your life have you witnessed divine power at the hand of a man of God? In what experience have you witnessed the merging of earth and heaven? What movement occurred from action to contemplation? from contemplation to action?

**Prayer**: As you live, O LORD, you answered the prayer of your prophet Elisha and restored life to the dead son of the Shunammite couple. Grant me a deep trust that all will be well for me today, tomorrow, and forever and ever. Amen.

## PURIFIED STEW

**Scripture**: "[Elisha] said, '. . . [B[ring some flour.' He threw it into the pot, and said, 'Serve the people and let them eat.' And there was nothing harmful in the pot." (2 Kgs 4:41)

**Read**: 2 Kings 4:38–41

**Reflection**: Just like he purified the spring of water near Jericho with salt (2 Kgs 2:19–22), so Elisha purifies a pot of stew with flour. The prophet has made his way to Gilgal, and there is a famine, just like there was a famine caused by drought in Elijah's time (1 Kgs 17:12). After teaching a company of prophets, he tells them to put the large pot on the fire and make stew for them to eat. In order to fill the pot, one of the prophets goes out to gather herbs. He finds a wild vine with gourds, which he picks, brings back, cuts up, and puts into the stew. While eating the stew, the prophets tell Elisha, "O man of God, there is death in the pot!" (2 Kgs 4:40b) What they mean is that the gourds in the stew are poisonous; and if they eat the stew, they will die. Elisha requests some flour, which he throws into the pot to purify the stew. After he does so, he instructs the company of prophets to eat the stew, because there was no longer anything harmful in the pot.

Not only does Elisha use a common item—flour—to purify the stew, but he again demonstrates that the divine is channeled through the ordinary. Previously it was salt; now it is flour which demonstrates the LORD's power at work in his prophet. Elisha also shows the company of prophets that they must trust him as a man of God. The famine in the land represents the famine of trust that exists in the company of prophets. Contemplative spirituality focuses on letting go of what one does not think is possible. In this case, the company of prophets does not think that it is possible to remove the poison from a pot of stew. Elisha demonstrates that letting go, letting God take over, can make the impossible possible!

In the Christian Bible (New Testament), Jesus of Nazareth teaches the same lesson to his followers. He tells them not to worry about life, what they will eat, what they will wear. In fact, by worrying they cannot add a single hour to their lives. According to Jesus, God already knows what people need. All they have to do is strive for God's kingdom and righteousness, and all they need will be given to them. If God takes care of the birds in the air and the lilies in the field—both of which do nothing to preserve their existence—then certainly God will take care of people, just like he took care of the company of prophets being taught by Elisha (Matt 6:25–33; Luke 12:22–31). Likewise, in the Longer Ending of Mark's Gospel, Jesus tells his disciples that signs will accompany them on their missionary journeys. One sign is the ability to pick up snakes in their hands and drink any deadly thing and not be hurt (Mark 16:18). In other words, they have nothing to worry about.

In a culture characterized by consumerism, many people spend more time protecting what they have bought rather than trusting God. Homes full of things need storage facilities to keep other things. Doubly locked doors, bared windows, and outdoor and indoor surveillance cameras help calm fears that someone will break in and take something. There is also a fear of not having enough, so there are lines to buy gasoline, bottled water, and other supplies. Even the fear of death can be calmed by buying life insurance. Those who spend time in solitary contemplation realize that nothing can guarantee life; the only one who can provide life is God. And all that people can do is trust him! Elisha teaches this. Jesus teaches the same. Out of contemplation, one begins to recognize that all the really matters is trust of God. Using some flour, Elisha tells the company of prophets to trust him, a man of God, who brings the divine power to preserve them.

**Journal/Meditation**: What ordinary item in your home is a vehicle to channel the divine to you? In what specific ways do you trust God to take care of your needs? What did you once think impossible became possible because you trusted God? How does a consumer culture influence your spirituality?

**Prayer**: O LORD, your prophet Elisha taught the company of prophets to trust your power channeled through the flour he threw into the poisoned pot of stew. Through contemplation, lead me into deeper levels of faith that all my striving may be toward your kingdom now and forever. Amen.

## LOAVES

**Scripture**: "Elisha said, 'Give [the twenty loaves of barley and fresh ears of grain] to the people and let them eat.' But his servant said, 'How can I set this before a hundred people?'" (2 Kgs 4:42b–43a)

**Read**: 2 Kings 4:42–44

**Reflection**: An unnamed man brings the first fruits of his harvest to the LORD, represented by the person of Elisha. Paradoxically, the man, who knows Elisha to be a man of God, comes from Baal-shalishah, a suburb of Shalishah and a town dedicated to Baal, a fertility god! In other words, a man brings the first fruits from the town named for the fertility god to the man of God, Elisha, who worships the LORD! He brings twenty small loaves of bread made from barley and some fresh ears of grain in a sack. Because there is famine in Gilgal (2 Kgs 4:38), and consequently lack of food, Elisha instructs the man to give the food to the people—the company of prophets—to eat. Elisha's servant, Gehazi, asks him how one hundred people (prophets) can be fed by so little food. All Elisha replies is this: "Give it to the people and let them eat, for thus says the LORD, 'They shall eat and have some left'" (2 Kgs 4:43b). Elisha's servant does as he is told, and all one hundred people (prophets) eat; there is some left over "according to the word of the LORD" (2 Kgs 4:44).

First, it is important to note the model for this story, found in the Hebrew Bible (Old Testament) book of Exodus. Elisha is being presented as a new Moses, who reports to the Israelites that the LORD was going to rain bread from heaven for them to eat (Exod 16:4, 12). In the mornings after the dew lifts, the Israelites gather a fine flaky substance from the surface of the wilderness; they name it manna (Exod 16:14–15, 31; Deut 8:4, 16). And they eat the manna for the forty years they spend in the wilderness (Exod 16:35; Josh 5:2). Elisha is held in the same esteem as Moses because the LORD works through both of them to provide food for people to eat. Psalm 78 rehearses the Exodus event, while it seems to have the narrative about Elisha also in mind: "[The LORD] rained down on [the Israelites] manna to eat, and gave them the grain of heaven" (Ps 78:24).

This same narrative about the LORD feeding one hundred people with twenty small barley loaves through Elisha becomes the basis for the multiple narratives of Jesus feeding hundreds in the Christian Bible (New Testament). Mark's Gospel contains two such stories, as does Matthew's Gospel. Luke's Gospel and John's Gospel have only one. Five loaves and two fish (equaling seven, the number indicating completeness) feed five (indicating gift, grace) thousand men with twelve baskets full of leftovers (Mark 6:35–44; Matt 14:15–21; Luke 9:12–17). After the crowd has been with Jesus for three (meaning divine) days, seven loaves feed four (referencing the earth) thousand people with seven baskets full of leftovers (Mark 8:1–9; Matt 15:32–38). The Johannine edition of the narrative (John 6:3–13) is set near Passover and is more elaborate than the stories found in Mark's Gospel and repeated in Matthew's Gospel and Luke's Gospel. However, John's Gospel specifically refers to five barley loaves and two fish (John 6:9) and later only the five barley loaves (John 6:13), clearly relying upon the account found in 2 Kings 4:42–44. The five barley loaves and two fish feed five thousand people (John 6:10) with twelve baskets of leftovers (John 6:13).

In a consumer culture, only the spiritually contemplative recognize the truth that out of a little there comes plenty. God takes the little bit that people have—like twenty, five, or seven barley loaves—and multiplies them. A ten-dollar check given to a charity that helps victims of natural disasters, like hurricanes, earthquakes, and floods, can turn that check into thirty dollars of clean-up. A twenty-dollar bill handed over to a food bank or homeless shelter can become food for four people for seven days. Organizations that build homes and schools in nations too poor to supply those for their citizens can turn one hundred dollars into five hundred dollars worth of building supplies. Elisha reminds all that the word of the LORD, once spoken and contemplated, results in the abundant activity of feeding the hungry.

**Journal/Meditation**: What experience of your life began with a little and resulted in plenty? How was God at work in your experience? How does living in a consumer culture affect you seeing the truth that out of a little God can bring plenty? Give specific examples.

**Prayer**: You spoke your word, O LORD, to your prophet Elisha that your prophets should eat of the barley loaves and have some left, and after they ate they had some left. Out of the little that you have entrusted to my stewardship bring plenty that I may learn your truth and live according to it now and forever. Amen.

Elisha

## NAAMAN: PART 1

**Scripture**: "Naaman, commander of the army of the king of Aram, was a great man and in high favor with his master, because by him the LORD had given victory to Aram. The man, though a mighty warrior, suffered from leprosy." (2 Kgs 5:1)

**Read**: 2 Kings 5:1–5a

**Reflection**: In this five-act narrative, the reader is suddenly introduced to Naaman, general of the Aramean army for the king of Aram (modern Damascus in Syria). This great man is highly favored by his king because the LORD, Israel's God, has given great victory over Israel to Aram. Thus, the first paradox is revealed: The LORD has made his people's enemy great and given them victory over his own people! The second paradox is similar to the first: This great warrior, Naaman, has common leprosy, some type of infectious skin disease characterized by ulcers and white, scaly scabs.

The reader is also introduced to an unnamed little Israelite girl, who, in a slave-trader raid by the Arameans, was captured and serves Naaman's wife. The third paradox presents itself: The little slave girl tells her unnamed mistress about the prophet in Samaria, Elisha, whose fame reaches beyond Israel's borders and could cure Naaman of his leprosy. Naaman's wife tells him what the slave girl said, and Naaman, in turn, tells his king, who instructs him, a non-Israelite, to go see the Israelite prophet: the fourth paradox.

To facilitate this meeting, the king of Aram tells Naaman that he will write a letter to the king of Israel. This is the fifth paradox: one enemy unnamed king (of Aram) sends a letter to the other unnamed enemy king (of Israel) in the hope of having the one enemy king of Aram's general cured of leprosy. In other words, the king of Aram agrees that Naaman go see his enemy for help; this is the very enemy over whom the LORD gave victory to Naaman! He is going to seek a cure from the people he has defeated! Thus, Naaman sets out with much wealth to pay for his cure: ten talents of silver (about 756 pounds), six thousand shekels of gold (about 151 pounds), and ten sets of garments (about a closet full).

There is another paradox in the first act of this story. It is a little slave maid who recommends to the mighty Naaman that he go see Elisha. The little girl, who is whole, recommends that the not-whole Naaman seek a cure from Israel's famous prophet. Naaman's leprosy reflects his not-yet belief in Israel's God. The general is presented as one who is quick and full of action, but has no contemplation. The slave girl is full of contemplation;

thus, she, a seemingly minor character, plays a major role in the story. She is the wisdom character! The LORD, who had given victory to Naaman over his own people, is about to give him healing at the word of his own prophet. Thus, Israel's LORD is a universal God; he cares about all people, even his people's enemy!

In the Lukan Jesus' first discourse in the synagogue in Nazareth on the sabbath, he reflects on the fact that no prophet is accepted in his hometown. One example he uses is that of Elisha. Jesus states: "There were . . . many lepers in Israel in the time of the prophet Elisha, and none of them was cleansed except Naaman the Syrian" (Luke 4:27). In other words, the Lukan Jesus interprets his people's questioning of his wisdom as rejection. He sees the healing of Naaman through Elisha as God's judgment against Israel.

There is deep truth in paradox, but it can be mined only with careful contemplation. Such a self-contradictory statement, like Israel's LORD gives victory to Israel's enemy, requires a lot of thought. How can a great warrior also be a leper? A little slave girl, representing wholeness, is the messenger to the free and mighty Naaman, representing un-wholeness. A non-Israelite, Naaman, goes to see an Israelite prophet, Elisha. A king writes to one he has defeated seeking a cure for his general. What the first act of the Naaman-Elisha story illustrates is that God works through paradox; he removes the contradictions, the dualities, and the opposites and replaces them with himself. Through solitary contemplation, one comes to see the unity of all things that exists in the mind of the LORD.

**Journal/Meditation**: Of what paradox are you aware in your life? What truth does it reveal to you? In what specific ways is God at work in your paradox bringing together the contradictions, dualities, and opposites and replacing them with himself?

**Prayer**: O LORD, you give victory to the enemy of your people, you give leprosy to a great warrior, and you give wisdom to a little slave girl in order to reveal your truth to all people. Through contemplation, help me to understand your paradoxes and to see the wisdom of your ways today, tomorrow, and forever. Amen.

## NAAMAN: PART 2

**Scripture**: ". . . Naaman came with his horses and chariots, and halted at the entrance of Elisha's house. Elisha sent a messenger to him, saying,

'Go, wash in the Jordan seven times, and your flesh shall be restored and you shall be clean.'" (2 Kgs 5:9–10)

**Read**: 2 Kings 5:5b–12

**Reflection**: Along with his horses laden with wealth, Naaman brings the letter written by the unnamed king of Aram to the unnamed king of Israel. Naaman did not know what his master's letter said to the king of Israel: "When this letter reaches you, know that I have sent to you my servant Naaman, that you may cure him of his leprosy" (2 Kgs 5:6). In other words, the king of Aram has misunderstood what Naaman told him. Naaman wants to see Elisha, but his master has sent him to the king of Israel. The king of Israel's response to reading the letter is to tear his clothes, an act of humility. Then he declares that he is not God; he cannot determine death or life; he cannot heal a man of leprosy. In fact, he declares, he thinks that the king of Aram is trying to pick a fight with him by sending Naaman to him for a cure.

News spreads fast in the ancient world, at least in its stories! Elisha hears that the king of Israel has torn his clothes, and he sends him a message. He wants the king to send Naaman to him so that Naaman learns that there is a prophet in Israel. So, Naaman brings his retinue to Elisha's doorstep, but the prophet doesn't even come out of his house. He sends a messenger to tell Naaman to go wash seven times in the Jordan River and he will be healed. However, Naaman is angry; he wants to see Elisha call on the name of the LORD and wave his hand over the leprosy to cure him. Furthermore, Naaman knows that the rivers in Damascus—Abana, Phapar—are cleaner than the Jordan. So, he goes away in a rage.

What Naaman misses is the presence of the LORD in Elisha's direction to go wash seven times in the Jordan River. Seven is a sacred number composed of three (representing the divine) and four (representing the earth). In other words, heaven is united to earth in the river water; healing awaits Naaman if he does what Elisha tells him to do. Naaman also misses the importance of the Jordan River: Joshua crossed it on dry ground with the priests bearing the ark of the covenant standing in the middle and dividing it; Elijah crossed it by rolling up his mantle and striking it, causing it to divide so he could cross on dry ground; Elisha crossed it on dry ground by wielding Elijah's mantle, which caused it to divide. All those crossings of the Jordan are meant to echo the parting and crossing of the Sea of Reeds under the extended hand of Moses. The LORD loves to part water so that his people can cross on dry ground! It's not that the Jordan River is cleaner than those in Damascus, it is that it is filled with the divine presence.

Naaman is upset because he does not get for what he is looking. He wants flare. He wants Elisha to make a dramatic exit from his home. He wants Elisha to call on the name of the LORD. He wants Elisha to wave his hand over the leprosy and watch it disappear. But, of course, Elisha does none of those actions. Elisha functions out of contemplation. Naaman functions out of activity. Naaman's perspective must change; he needs to see differently. Once his awareness about how he sees is changed, then what he sees will also change. Awareness is the result of contemplation.

When a person looks for a salt shaker, he or she usually finds it on a table or in a cabinet; thus, no one opens the refrigerator to find it. But what if that is where someone stores it? When looking for a carton of milk, a person goes to the refrigerator, unless someone decided to put it in a cabinet. How many times has a lost item been found when one is no longer looking for it, all because a person is seeing differently? How a person sees is what a person sees! One often finds for what he or she is searching but fails to see all else around it. This is the stance of Naaman after Elisha tells him to wash seven times in the Jordan River.

**Journal/Meditation**: When have you acted like Naaman? When have you entertained a new activity that first seemed reasonably absurd only to discover the divine presence? In what odd place have you found God? What experience of your life shows you that awareness is the result of contemplation?

**Prayer**: O LORD, through Elisha, your prophet, you sent Naaman to wash seven times in the Jordan River, where he would encounter your presence. Make me aware of your company in all the people and things I encounter today. You live forever and ever. Amen.

## NAAMAN: PART 3

**Scripture**: "... [Naaman's] servants approached and said to him, 'Father, if the prophet had commanded you to do something difficult, would you not have done it?'" (2 Kgs 5:13a)

**Read**: 2 Kings 5:13–14

**Reflection**: While he is in a rage because he didn't get what he expected from Elisha, Naaman, the Syrian army general, is unreasonable. However, his lowly servants step forward and present a reasonable argument to this great man. They make him aware that if Elisha had instructed him to do something difficult, he would have done it. He has to agree that he would have done any difficult thing Elisha imposed on him. Well, his servants conclude, if he would have done the difficult thing, how much more reasonable is it for him to do the simple thing, namely, to wash and be clean? Naaman, whom the respectful servants address as father, cannot present a counter argument to their reasoning. The paradox of the lowly servants possessing wisdom cannot be missed by the paradox of the great general's unreasonableness. In other words, those who should be ignorant, the servants, are actually the smarter. He who should be smart, Naaman, is ignorant. Wisdom is not always found where it is presumed to be! Servants become the means for Naaman to acquire wisdom!

So, following Elisha's instruction, Naaman walks down to the Jordan River and immerses himself in it seven times. And just as the man of God had told him, he walks out of the water with his flesh restored as if he were a young boy again. His leprosy is gone. Naaman must be totally overwhelmed at this change, which occurred without Elisha's presence, without the man of God calling on the name of the LORD, and without the prophet waving his hand over the leprosy. Simply plunging seven times in the divine, flowing water is enough to engender Naaman's cure!

The same scenario is found in the Christian Bible (New Testament) account of Jesus healing a leper. In Mark's Gospel, a leper finds Jesus, kneels at his feet, and begs him to make him clean. Jesus merely stretches out his hand and, making himself unclean, touches the leper, telling him to be clean. Immediately the leprosy leaves the man, and he is clean (Mark 1:40–42). The story is also found in Matthew's Gospel in a condensed form (Matt 8:2–3) and in Luke's Gospel in a slightly rewritten account (Luke 5:12–13). The author of Luke's Gospel also presents a story about Jesus healing ten lepers merely by sending them to the priests (Luke 17:12–19). This account has been clearly influenced by the account of Elisha sending Naaman to wash in the Jordan River. Like Elisha does nothing extraordinary, Jesus merely sends the ten lepers to the ancient health department quarantine representatives—the priests—who determine that they were made clean on their way to see them. One of the ten returns to Jesus to praise God; interestingly, he was a Samaritan, an outcast, a foreigner, similar in stature to Naaman from a typical Israelite point of view. Furthermore, Jesus praises the foreigner's faith, a faith that will be proclaimed by Naaman in the next part of his story.

# From Contemplation to Action

Naaman goes to the Jordan River in a state of contemplation as a result of his servants urging him to observe the simple activity that Elisha had given him. The servants invite their master to think about the bigger picture, to see a wider perspective, and then to act upon what he reflects. In solitude, Naaman comes to realize that the simple is the best. The LORD employs simple means—plunging into the water—to enact Naaman's double cure. Not only is his skin disease removed, but his inability to believe is also removed. Indeed, while "the LORD is in his holy temple," and "all the earth [should] keep silence before him" (Hab 2:20), he is also present in the Jordan River, where Naaman experiences his healing hand in silence.

One of the hardest facts for many believers is that God uses the ordinary to reveal himself. It is not that the LORD is absent; it is that people are not aware of his presence. A simple shower can make one aware of the divine, healing presence. Standing at the kitchen sink and washing the dishes can make a person aware of the divine, cleansing presence. Likewise, doing the laundry, brushing teeth over the bathroom sink, and flushing the toilet—all simple activities—are charged with the divine. Awareness takes time; awareness evolves in silence.

**Journal/Meditation**: When have you experienced the divine presence while doing something simple? In what odd place have you found wisdom? Who was your teacher? Where do you find the silence that makes you aware of God?

**Prayer**: LORD, you can be found in your holy temples and in all you have created. Grant that I may recognize your presence in all people and things and join all the earth in keeping silence before you forever and ever. Amen.

## NAAMAN: PART 4

**Scripture**: ". . . [Naaman] returned to the man of God, he and all his company; he came and stood before him and said, 'Now I know that there is no God in all the earth except in Israel; please accept a present from your servant.'" (2 Kgs 5:15)

**Read**: 2 Kings 5:15–19a

**Reflection**: As soon as Naaman is cured of his leprosy, he returns to Elisha, the man of God. Naaman has gone emotionally from rage to health. Furthermore, he has gone from disbelief to faith. And he professes his faith before Elisha and his retinue, declaring that there is no God on the earth except the LORD in Israel. In fact, Naaman quotes the faith of Israel: "Hear, O Israel: The LORD is our God, the LORD alone" (Deut 6:4). The paradox is overwhelming; the commander of Aram's armed forces, a worshiper of Hadad Ramman (Rimmon)—the thunder and weather god of Syria—declares that the only God is the LORD! Hadad was Syria's god, and Ramman was his title. In this story about Elisha, he is derogatorily referred to as Rimmon (meaning *pomegranate*). There may have been two different gods, Hadad and Ramman (Rimmon), who were syncretized into a single deity and in fertility rites functioned as the dying and rising god of vegetation.

Furthermore, Naaman wants to give a gift to Elisha to thank him for the cure. The general brought silver, gold, and garments with him for this very purpose. Elisha, using the typical biblical formula, declares, "As the LORD lives, whom I serve, I will accept nothing!" (2 Kgs 5:16a) Even though Naaman encourages the man of God to accept something, he refuses all of the commander's gifts. Why? Because it is not Elisha who has cured Naaman of his leprosy; it is the LORD who has made him clean and whole again. And the LORD needs no silver, gold, or clothes! It takes Naaman a moment to contemplate this, but when he does, he realizes that instead of offering a present to Elisha, he should ask him for other gifts.

Thus, Naaman's first request is for two mule-loads of Israelite earth to haul back to Aram. At first this seems like a very strange request. Naaman, thinking that the LORD can be worshiped only on Israelite ground, wants the soil so that he can offer burnt offerings to the LORD on Israelite earth! While the text does not state that Elisha granted his request, the presumption is that he did. This desire to have two mule-loads of Israelite soil resembles the practice in El Sanctuario de Chimayo in New Mexico. People visit the adobe church in order to scoop from a pit in the church floor a reddish soil which, after taking it home, they rub on afflicted areas of their bodies, sprinkle on food, or brew in tea with the hope of a cure of whatever ails them. It is also similar to those who visit the shrine of Our Lady of Lourdes in Lourdes, France, and bathe in or fill a bottle of water from the spring in the Grotto of Massabielle which, after taking it home, they apply to their bodies and/or drink with the hope of a cure for their illnesses.

Naaman's second request is for pardon. Naaman explains that he must accompany his master, the king of Aram, when he goes into Hadad Ramman's (Rimmon) temple, in which he bows to a god he knows does not exist. In other words, now that he believes that the LORD is the only God, his position as army general places him in jeopardy. Thus, he needs to be pardoned for this required devotion before he even gets home and finds himself in that situation. Elisha grants his second request by merely sending him home in peace. Elisha knows that the LORD has seen Naaman's faith and no matter what his activity may be, Naaman believes in him.

This fourth part of the Naaman narrative contemplates the boundlessness of the LORD. God healed the general's leprosy. The LORD brought Naaman to faith in the only God in all the earth. God gave Naaman two mule-loads of Israelite soil. The LORD pardoned him for pretending to worship a god that does not exist. Contemplating the LORD's boundlessness, generosity, and munificence, Naaman understands that all gifts come from him and all people belong to him. This is quite a step to take for the great army commander of Aram.

**Journal/Meditation**: Have you been cured through the use of sacred soil or holy water? Explain. Do you expect a reward for a cure that has occurred to another through your healing word or hand? Where do you find God's boundlessness in your life? What do you request of the LORD this day after recognizing his graciousness?

**Prayer**: As you live, O LORD, whom I serve, I willingly accept your underserved gifts of healing, pardon, earth, and water that give me life. Let this prayer be one of gratitude to you now and forever and ever. Amen.

## NAAMAN: PART 5

**Scripture**: "... [W]hen Naaman had gone from him a short distance, Gehazi, the servant of Elisha the man of God, thought, 'My master has let that Aramean Naaman off too lightly by not accepting from him what he offered. As the LORD lives, I will run after him and get something out of him.'" (2 Kgs 5:19b–20)

**Read**: 2 Kings 5:19b–27

**Reflection**: Just when the reader things that the narrative concerning Naaman and Elisha must be finished, there is act five! Gehazi, Elisha's servant, introduced earlier in the story about the Shunammite couple (2 Kgs 4:11, 25b, 31, 36), begins to judge Elisha's refusal of Naaman's gifts. Basically, he says to himself that Elisha was wrong to let Naaman return to Aram without leaving behind some of the silver, gold, and garments. So, he runs to catch up with Naaman's chariot, which the general stops when he sees Gehazi following him. Thus, Gehazi's first mistake is judging Elisha.

Gehazi's second mistake is lying to Naaman. He tells him that Elisha has sent him to say that two members of a company of prophets have arrived, and they could use a talent of silver and two changes of clothing. Out of his generosity, Naaman gives Gehazi two talents of silver, two sets of clothes, and two servants to carry the wealth in front of Gehazi back to his master's home, where he stores the goods and dismisses the servants to return to Naaman.

Gehazi's third mistake is standing before Elisha and lying to him. After Elisha asks him where he's been, he declares that he has not left the house. However, the clairvoyant Elisha tells him that he went with Gehazi in spirit when he approached Naaman and asked for money and clothing. Overexaggerating Gehazi's request, in order to make his point, Elisha states that Gehazi also asked for olive orchards, vineyards, sheep, oxen, and male and female slaves! What began as Gehazi's judgment of Elisha has grown into two lies and results in Elisha's judgment of Gehazi.

Because Gehazi's evil is three-fold, Elisha pronounces divine judgment upon him. The leprosy that left Naaman comes to Gehazi and his descendants forever. And so Gehazi leaves Elisha's presence covered in white-as-snow leprosy. Thus, the final paradox is presented: A pagan leper, who is cured of his leprosy and professes faith in the LORD, is set beside Gehazi, the servant of the man of God who dishonors Elisha, the LORD, and is cursed with leprosy. Naaman should not have been cured, but he was. Gehazi should not have lied, but he did. Naaman should not have professed faith in the LORD, but he did. Gehazi should have had faith in the LORD, but he did not.

This paradoxical account is echoed in the Christian Bible (New Testament) Acts of the Apostles. After the author describes the unanimity of the first Christian community—particularly how the members sold their property and donated the proceeds to meet the needs of other members—he narrates a tale about a couple named Ananias and Sapphira (Acts 5:1–11). The couple sells a piece of property and lies to the community by indicating that they are giving all they got from the sale to the apostles for the good of all. However, they have held back some of the proceeds. Peter, who is like Elisha in the story above, accuses Ananias of lying to the Holy Spirit and to God before he falls down dead! Three divine hours later, Sapphira comes looking for Ananias, and Peter accuses her of lying to the Holy Spirit and God. She falls down and dies at Peter's feet.

## From Contemplation to Action

The point of both narratives is that there is danger in judging and lying to a prophet or to the leader of the Christian community. Such a message is not easily heard by those who prefer to tell others what they think they want to hear instead of telling the truth. Children tell their parents that they have finished all their homework and, therefore, can play video games, when they have only finished a part of it. Employees tell employers that they were sick two days last week, when they only wanted two days free to sleep, shop, or watch a game on TV. Patients tell their doctors that they are taking their medication regularly, when the truth is that they take it only a few days a week. Are those not forms of lying? There is danger in lying, because the omniscient LORD knows the truth!

**Journal/Meditation**: In your life, what experience of judging another led to lies? In what ways were you punished for your lies? Do you think it is OK to tell little white lies? Why or why not? What is at stake when lying?

**Prayer**: You go with me in spirit throughout my life, O LORD, telling me not to judge and inviting me to speak the truth from my heart. Send the Holy Spirit to purify my mind and heart so that I make your truth known to the world now and forever. Amen.

## FLOATING AX HEAD

**Scripture**: "... [T]he man of God [, Elisha,] said, 'Where did [the ax head] fall?' When [the feller] showed him the place, he cut off a stick, and threw it in [the Jordan River], and made the iron float." (2 Kgs 6:6)

**Read**: 2 Kings 6:1–7

**Reflection**: Everyone knows that iron does not float on water. Everyone knows that except Elisha, of course! While cutting trees near the Jordan River in order to build a place to live for the company of prophets under Elisha's charge, one prophet's ax head flies off the handle and falls into the river. The situation is further compounded by the fact that the ax is borrowed; in justice it needs to be found and restored to its owner. All Elisha needs to know is where it entered the Jordan. Once the prophet shows the man of God the spot, Elisha cuts a stick, throws it into the river, and the ax head floats to the top. The prophet, who had lost it, picks up the iron floating on the water. Iron floating on water is a paradox, of course.

This short narrative about another wonder at the hands of Elisha follows the same literary form and recalls his purifying the spring near Jericho with salt (2 Kgs 2:19–22), his multiplying of the oil in the jar (2 Kgs

2:4:1–7), his purifying the pot of stew containing poisoned gourds with flour (2 Kgs 4:38–41), and his multiplication of twenty barley loaves to feed one hundred people (2 Kgs 4:42–44). An ordinary item—salt, oil, flour, barley loaves, and stick—becomes the means for the manifestation of the divine presence at the words and deeds of the LORD's prophet.

Another interesting paradox is also found in this short narrative. According to the Hebrew Bible (Old Testament) Book of Deuteronomy, during siege warfare, soldiers may not destroy a town's trees by wielding an ax against them (Deut 20:19). In the next verse, this directive is tempered when soldiers are told that they can destroy only the trees that they know do not bear food. Only non-fruit-bearing trees can be cut down for use in building siege works against towns that make war (Deut 20:20). The purpose of this directive is to curb the devastation of siege warfare. Thus, when Elisha gives permission to the company of prophets to cut trees growing near the Jordan River, he is violating the prohibition. The prophets are building a bigger house; they are not involved in siege warfare and, therefore, ineligible to cut any trees!

The focus of this account is not on tree cutting but on ax floating. Another mystical wonder appears at the words and deeds of Elisha. However, in this case the prophet ends up violating the LORD's own directive in the Book of Deuteronomy about cutting trees. Sometimes a law, rule, or guide must be negated for the greater good. Does a husband violate the law when he drives way over the posted speed limit to get his pregnant and in-labor wife to the hospital? Does a woman break a rule when she works seven hours one day and nine the next day and writes eight each day on her time sheet? Does a child break the guide that no sweets can be eaten before dinner when a grandparent hands him or her a small bag of chocolates and says to try one? Yes, Elisha makes the ax head float, but he also violates the LORD's commandment about not cutting trees in order to provide a bigger house for the company of prophets under his charge.

**Journal/Meditation**: What experience in your life dictated that for the greater good you needed to violate a law, rule, or guide? How was the divine manifested to you? What was the sign of divine presence even though you may have violated one of the LORD's laws, rules, or guides?

**Prayer**: LORD, through your prophet Elisha, you worked wonders for the company of prophets entrusted to his care. Work similar wonders, I pray, through my words and deeds; grant that they be for the greater good of all your people now and forever. Amen.

From Contemplation to Action

## ALL-KNOWING

**Scripture:** ". . . Elisha prayed: 'O LORD, please open his eyes that he may see.' So the LORD opened the eyes of the servant, and he saw; the mountain was full of horses and chariots of fire all around Elisha." (2 Kgs 6:17)

**Read:** 2 Kings 6:8–23

**Reflection:** This section of the narrative about Elisha can be divided easily into five acts. The first act features the king of Aram taking counsel with his officers; he is attempting to determine who the insider spy is that notifies the king of Israel where the Arameans are going to establish their camp. Clairvoyant Elisha, the man of God, is the person who divines the Aramean information and passes it on to the king of Israel. Elisha does this several times, and every time he is correct. This is because he sits alone in silence when the LORD imposes silence upon him in contemplation (Lam 3:28).

In act two, the king of Aram again calls his officers and asks them to identify the informant. They tell the king that it is not anyone in the Aramean army, but it is Elisha, the prophet in Israel, who informs the king of Israel of the words the Aramean king speaks in confidence to his men. The king is overjoyed to have that information, and he instructs his men to find Elisha, capture him, and bring him back to him. Aramean horses and chariots—a great army—head to Dothan, where surveillance indicates that is where Elisha has gone. The army surrounds the city.

Meanwhile, act three takes place. Early in the morning, one of Elisha's attendants in Dothan sees the army with horses and chariots all around the city. In other words, the city is under siege by the king of Aram. After telling Elisha about what he saw, he asks his master about their next move. Elisha quiets him, tells him not to be afraid, and reports that there are more soldiers with them than with the king of Aram. Understandably, Elisha's servant disbelieves. So, Elisha prays to the LORD asking him to open the eyes of his servant to see that the mountain is full of horses and chariots of fire all around Elisha. The LORD grants Elisha's request. Of course, the horses and chariots of fire are meant to remind the reader that Elisha is a new Elijah (2 Kgs 2:11). Furthermore, the fiery horses and chariots represent the enveloping care and protection of God for his prophet (2 Kgs 13:14). According to Psalm 34, "The angel of the LORD encamps around those who fear him, and delivers them" (Ps 34:7). Or, as the LORD declares through the prophet Zechariah, ". . . I will encamp at my house as a guard, so that no one shall march to and fro; no oppressor shall again overrun them, for now I have seen with my own eyes" (Zech 9:8).

Act four of this narrative features the Arameans attacking Dothan because they cannot see the army of the LORD of hosts. Again, Elisha prays to the LORD, asking him to strike all of the Aramean army with blindness. God does as Elisha asks, so that now the people blind to the LORD are also physically blind and cannot capture Elisha! In fact, Elisha functions as a typical biblical trickster. Since the soldiers are blind, they cannot recognize the man of God. Elisha tells them that they have gotten lost, and Dothan is not the correct city. He goes so far as to invite them to follow him, telling them that he will bring them to the man they seek. Thus, they follow him to Samaria, the capital of Israel!

Once the Aramean army follows Elisha to Samaria, Israel, act five begins with the prophet's prayer to the LORD to open their eyes so they can see where they are. God does as Elisha requests. When the king of Israel sees that his enemy has been delivered into his hands in his own capital city, he asks Elisha if he should kill them. Paradoxically, Elisha tells him that he should do no harm to his enemy because he did not capture them. Again, paradoxically, Elisha instructs the king to show them hospitality by providing them with a great feast of food and water and then letting them return home. After this, the Arameans stop raiding into the land of Israel.

Elisha's prayers to the LORD are heard. As the world's greatest wireless connection, prayer is finding one's self in God. This narrative contains three of Elisha's prayers to indicate that the LORD is hearing him and answering him. He prays that his servant might see the horses and chariots of fire surrounding him. He asks the LORD to blind the Aramean army, and, after tricking them to follow him into Samaria, he asks the LORD to restore their sight. Through prayer, Elisha has everything under control because God and he are united; they function as a team. Elisha is the cause of the Aramean invasion, but he is also the cause of the rescue of Israel by the LORD. Furthermore, Elisha prefers to teach his enemy a lesson rather than slaughter them within the gates of Samaria. Out of his contemplation, he instructs that three divine, hospitable activities be done. The enemy army is to be given water and food and permitted to leave unharmed. In the Christian Bible (New Testament), Elisha's hospitality becomes Jesus' instruction to his disciples to love their enemies (Matt 5:44; Luke 6:26). They should expect nothing in return, but they will be rewarded by the Most High (Luke 6:35), just like Israel was rewarded with no more Aramean raids. In Paul's

Letter to the Romans, he follows Elisha's activity by instructing his readers to feed their enemies and to give drink to them. By doing so, they will heap burning coals on their heads (Rom 12:20); this means that they will defeat their enemies with hospitality.

**Journal/Meditation:** Have you ever been blind to the LORD's presence? Who helped you see? What enemy have you defeated with hospitality? How does silent contemplation enable you to know what act to take? How does God take care of you?

**Prayer:** O LORD, please open my eyes that I may see your horses and chariots of fire all around me. And grant that the hospitality I show to my enemies may heap burning coals on their heads. All praise be yours now and forever. Amen.

## SAMARIA UNDER SIEGE: PART 1

**Scripture:** ". . . Elisha was sitting in his house, and the elders were sitting with him. Before the messenger arrived, Elisha said to the elders, 'Are you aware that this murderer has sent someone to take off my head. When the messenger comes, see that you shut the door and hold it closed against him. Is not the sound of his master's feet behind him?'" (2 Kgs 6:32bcde)

**Read:** 2 Kings 6:24—7:2

**Reflection:** Even though the last verse of the previous narrative stated that the Arameans no longer came raiding into the land of Israel (2 Kgs 6:23b), sometime later, according to the next story, King Ben-hadad of Aram mustered his army, marched to Samaria—the capital of Israel—and laid siege to it. Laying siege to a city means that the walls surrounding and protecting the city are themselves surrounded by the enemy. This creates a paradox; the walls meant to protect the city become the means for the city's demise. In other words, the walls that are meant to keep out the enemy simultaneously keep in the citizens. The siege maneuver cuts off the food supply to Samaria. Thus, people within the walls are eating donkeys' heads, selling for almost two pounds of silver, and a fourth of a quart of dove's dung selling for less than three ounces of silver. In other words, prices are astronomical because food is scarce!

The situation is so dire that as the unnamed king of Israel is walking along the city walls to see what is going on with his enemy outside, a woman spots him and asks him for help. He tells her, "Let the LORD help you" (2 Kgs 6:27a). Besides obviously blaming the LORD for the siege he is experiencing, the king also declares that even he has no more resources from the threshing floor—a raised area where grain was separated from the hull—or from the wine press—where grapes were squeezed for their juice to make wine. Nevertheless, he seeks to know her complaint.

The unnamed woman's legal complaint further illustrates the direness of the situation. She and another woman in the city had reached an agreement that they would eat her son one day and the other woman's son the next day. In other words, food is so scarce that the inhabitants have reverted to cannibalism. After eating the son of the woman who is filing a complaint with the king, the other woman hid her son and refused to kill, cook, and eat him. Like King Solomon of the past, this unnamed king must reach a decision (1 Kgs 3:16–28).

Upon hearing about the desperate straits that his people are enduring, the king tears his clothes as a sign of grief and loss to reveal that he has the sackcloth of mourning under them. Then, he swears that he is going to have Elisha's head removed from his body because—for some unknown reason—he blames the prophet as the LORD's representative for the siege of the city and the distress it has caused its citizens. This king is very much like King Ahab and Queen Jezebel, who sought Elijah's life (1 Kgs 19:3). Thus, the king dispatches a messenger to Elisha, who is sitting in his house with the elders of the people.

Before the messenger arrives clairvoyant Elisha—a characteristic of the prophet seen multiple times before—tells the elders that the king, whom Elisha refers to as a murderer, has sent a messenger to decapitate him. He instructs the elders not to open the door when the messenger arrives at Elisha's house. Before the man of God is finished speaking, however, the king's messenger arrives with the king behind him, declaring that the cause of the siege is the LORD. However, Elisha declares that his attributing the city's troubles to the LORD is in error. The next day, declares the prophet, the prices for food will go down. A measure of choice meal—about six and a half bushels—will cost only one shekel—two one hundredths (.02) of a pound of silver. Two measures of barley—thirteen bushels—will cost only one shekel also. Of course, Elisha is exaggerating that such a dramatic increase in food with lower prices will occur, but he is declaring that his word is the word of the LORD.

The king's captain recognizes the absurdity of Elisha's declaration during the present situation and states humorously, "Even if the LORD were to make windows in the sky, could such a thing happen?" (2 Kgs 7:2a) Because of his disbelieve, Elisha tells the captain that he will see this bounty occur, but he will not be able to share in it.

What the captain fails to recognize is that tiny changes can lead to big consequences. As the archangel Gabriel tells Mary of Nazareth, nothing is impossible with God (Luke 1:37). Because no one can know the future, except the LORD, no one can predict accurately what will occur, except for the man of God, Elisha. The message Elisha delivers is trust that God will act. Elisha delivers the message only after spending time in contemplation so that the word of God he speaks is, indeed, the word of the LORD. While trust in a culture that teaches one to trust only himself or herself is difficult, it is not impossible for those whose contemplation leads to action.

**Journal/Meditation**: What wall, fence, or other enclosure have you discovered to be paradoxical, that is, it keeps out others while also keeping you within? In your own experience, what did you once think impossible that became possible? Explain.

**Prayer**: O LORD, I need your help. Send your word to me, like you did to your prophet Elisha. After hearing it, give me the faith to follow it today, tomorrow, and forever. Amen.

## SAMARIA UNDER SIEGE: PART 2

**Scripture**: "... [T[he Lord had caused the Aramean army to hear the sound of chariots, and of horses, the sound of a great army, so that they said to one another, 'The king of Israel has hired the kings of the Hittites and the kings of Egypt to fight against us.' So they fled away in the twilight and abandoned their tents, their horses, and their donkeys leaving the camp just as it was, and fled for their lives." (2 Kgs 7:6–7)

**Read**: 2 Kings 7:3–20

**Reflection**: There are three acts to this second part of the story concerning the Aramean siege of Samaria. The first act opens with a story about four lepers who are outside the city gates because they are not permitted to be within them with any kind of skin disease. The story mentions four lepers to indicate that their activity is about to encompass their entire world. These outcasts outside the city gates evaluate their options and discover that they have three. The first option is that they can remain where they are until they die. The second option is they can attempt to enter the city, but there they will die because of the famine. Their third option is to desert to the Aramean camp where their enemies may kill them or spare their lives and give them food. In other words, the four lepers have nothing to lose; they are going to die one way or another!

After determining that their third option gives them a glimmer of staying alive, they choose to leave the city walls of Samaria and walk to the Aramean camp at twilight. When they get there, they discover that no one is there; it is a ghost camp! The narrator of the story explains that the Lord has tricked the Arameans into hearing the sound of a great army and thinking that the unnamed king of Israel had hired mercenary armies to fight against them. Thus, before sunrise Israel's enemies fled for their lives and left their camp and its supplies—tents, horses, and donkeys—in place.

A similar story is narrated by the prophet Isaiah, who states that the LORD would put a spirit in the king of Assyria so that he would hear a rumor and return to his own land, leaving the city of Jerusalem without attacking its walls (Isa 37:7). Isaiah attributes the motivation for the Assyrians leaving to an angel of the LORD who strikes down one hundred eighty-five thousand Assyrians during the night. In the morning, all the dead bodies are discovered, and King Sennacherib of Assyria leaves Jerusalem and returns to Nineveh (Isa 37:36–37).

Upon finding the abandoned Aramean camp, the four leprous men take advantage of the situation. They enter a tent and find food, so they eat and drink. They also find silver, gold, and clothing, which they pick up, carry away, and hide in the woods. In other words, this is quite a treasure trove for lepers! After hiding their goods, they come back to the empty camp, enter another tent, find more of the same, and carry off more things and hide them. This first act is, literally, a rags-to-riches story!

However, in act two the lepers stop their activity in the abandoned Aramean camp, and they begin to contemplate their activity. They have already demonstrated their critical thinking skills by concluding that they had nothing to lose by deserting to the camp in the first place. After reflecting upon their actions, they conclude that they are doing wrong by not telling the starving citizens in the city about the supply of food they have discovered. In other words, if they stay silent until the next morning, the citizens will find out in the meantime, and they will be declared guilty of withholding this good news. They conclude that it is best to go to Samaria and tell the king what they have discovered.

The paradox of the lepers cannot go unmentioned. The very city that has made them outcasts because of their leprosy, the very city that will not let them inside the city walls for protection, is the city to which they go as messengers of freedom. They are the most unlikely of saviors to the very people who have put them in harm's way outside the city gates. The outcasts go back to the city gates to minister to the incasts! The filled outcasts bring the message of food and water to the famine-stricken people behind the city walls!

When they get to the city gates, they call the gatekeepers and tell them what they found in the Aramean camp: horses, donkeys, and tents. The gatekeepers in turn pass on the information to the king's household. After the king's servants report the good news to him, he declares that he thinks the abandoned camp is a trap. Knowing that the Israelites are starving, the Arameans have left the camp, but are hiding and waiting for everyone to come out of the city and capture them. One of the king's servants is not as sure of the trap as the king is. So, he proposes that two men take two of the five remaining horses and investigate the message relayed by the lepers. So, two men on horseback are dispatched to follow the Aramean army to be sure they have left the country. Indeed, the scouts follow the army all the way to the Jordan River, discovering clothes and equipment left by the side of the road all along the way. After their investigation they return to Samaria and verify the lepers' truth.

Act three of this account begins with the people leaving the city and plundering the Aramean camp. First, this activity reverses the famine that resulted in cannibalism earlier in the story (2 Kgs 6:28–29). Second, it also fulfills the man of God's words about a measure of choice meal being sold for a shekel and two measures of barley for a shekel, according to word of the LORD (2 Kgs 7:1, 18). The basic law of supply and demand that had previously caused extremely high prices during the famine is now the result of extremely low prices during plenty, paradoxically caused by the abundance of the enemy's camp. Third, Elisha had told the king's captain that he would not eat of the abundance ending the famine because of his lack of faith (2 Kgs 7:2, 19). The same captain was put in charge of the city gate by the king; he is trampled to death by the people who rush out of the city gate to get to the supplies of food and all else left behind by the Arameans when he opens the gate.

Elisha is one of those wise men who died to egocentricity when he was called by Elijah to succeed him. Death to ego is the core of transformation. That is what the captain cannot do. He cannot die to the seemingly rational belief that even if the LORD could make a window in the sky, the end of the famine and Elisha's prediction about abundant food is impossible. The captain does not speak out of contemplation; he knows only activity. As a man of God, Elisha contemplates the word of the LORD in solitude; he knows that activity flows out of contemplation. Furthermore, he bears witness to the wonders that God can do in those who trust him.

While everyone in Samaria has shrunk and continues to shrink the circle of compassion behind the city walls in an effort to fill themselves and so silence their fear of death, Elisha touches his own being—which is simultaneously a share in Divine Being—and functions as a steward of the LORD's gracious words. He helps those yearning for life to recognize that they are connected. Four leprous men—the least likely heroes, so outcast that they cannot enter the city—discover the LORD's defeat of the Aramean army and set in motion a chain of connectivity that leads to the end of famine and an abundance of enemy supplies! The distance between the lepers, the citizens, and the king is reduced to community, while the distance between Israel's enemies and unbelievers gets further apart. The LORD takes care of his people.

In a modern world, the truth taught by the three-act story remains. If people stop letting religious affiliation divide them, they can discover a community sharing Divine Being. If people stop letting sexual orientation divide them, they can discover a community of humanity created in the image of God. If people stop letting the color of skin divide them, they discover a community of diversity from the LORD's hand that enriches their lives. If Elisha can hold out hope in the midst of siege and famine, how can people today not hold out hope to each other in the midst of freedom and abundance?

**Journal/Meditation**: Who have been the most unlikely saviors in your lifetime of experiences? In what specific experiences of wonders of God have you discovered the LORD caring for you and your needs? In what specific ways have you died to egocentricity? How were you transformed?

**Prayer**: This is a day of good news, O LORD. I cannot be silent and wait until the morning light. I must tell of your marvelous wonders in my life that draw me ever closer to others and the divine being that we share. All praise be to you now and forever. Amen.

From Contemplation to Action

## SHUNAMMITE WOMAN AGAIN

**Scripture**: "At the end of . . . seven years, when the [Shunammite] woman returned from the land of the Philistines, she set out to appeal to the king for her house and her land." (2 Kgs 8:3)

**Read**: 2 Kings 8:1–6

**Reflection**: This six-verse account about the unnamed Shunammite woman continues Elisha's dealings with her. Thus, it probably followed the other material at 2 Kings 4:8–37 and got misplaced at its current location in the Second Book of Kings. The Shunammite woman and her husband had built a rooftop room for Elisha, who had promised her a son. The son died, but Elisha brought him back to life. This story presumes that the woman's husband is dead. Functioning as Elijah did before King Ahab (1 Kgs 17:1), Elisha informs the woman that the LORD has called for a famine for seven years. These complete seven years are similar to Elijah's divine three years (1 Kgs 17:1). Elisha instructs the owner of his room to leave the area and settle somewhere else where food and water can be found. She and the members of her household leave Israel and settle in enemy territory, the land of the Philistines. Biblically, one often finds safety while living among one's enemies! David is the best example of this; after defeating the Philistines many times, he went to live with them to escape the threats of King Saul (1 Sam 27:1).

After living among the Philistines for seven years, the Shunammite woman returns to Israel to discover that someone is squatting on her property and making a legal claim of ownership against her. Thus, she must appear to the unnamed king, who just by happenstance is speaking to Gehazi, Elisha's servant, when the woman presents herself to the king. There is no mention of Gehazi's leprosy (which had occurred after Naaman's healing) in this account, so some biblical scholars think this story may have come after Elisha's death instead of before it. Nevertheless, this story is about the same woman whose son Elisha restored to life, a wonder which Gehazi is rehearsing for the king when the woman appears. Gehazi identifies the woman to the king as being the owner of the property. This results in the king appointing an official to oversee the removal of the squatter and the restoration of her property to her in addition to the revenues from the fields that have accrued over the past seven years.

Even though it is Gehazi who verifies the woman's identity, it is Elisha who directed her to leave the land of Israel and live with the Philistines for seven years. Gehazi implores the king to enact justice, to give the

Shunammite woman what is due her, and the king appoints one of his officials to see that justice is enacted. Those who associate with Elisha prosper in every way, even while they live among their enemies!

Both Elisha and Gehazi invite contemplation that explores personal perception of others. Nowhere in the story does the woman refer to the Philistines as her enemy; that is a fact gleaned from other biblical accounts. Another person is an enemy because a person perceives him or her to be without contemplation or reflection on the other's activity or lack thereof. A panhandler may be perceived as an aggravating enemy by a driver of a car, but he or she may be homeless and in need of funds or rich and wanting to experience homelessness in North America. A person with a conceal-and-carry permit for a handgun may be perceived as an enemy fearing everyone, but he or she may have an ailment that makes him or her more vulnerable to robbery than most people. How many times have a few people in a traffic jam judged the person at the head of the line their enemy only to get there and discover that he or she has died at the wheel or in an accident? Without all the facts justice cannot be rendered accurately according to Elisha and Gehazi. Without all the facts justice should not be rendered at all. The one perceived to be the enemy may not be the enemy at all!

**Journal/Meditation**: What have been your experiences of justice? When have you discovered yourself naming enemies only to discover they were not enemies at all? Have you ever found safety while living among enemies? Explain.

**Prayer**: O LORD, through your prophet Elisha, you called for a famine, and he instructed his patroness to go and live with her enemies. After finding sustenance with them for seven years, she returned and you gave her justice. Grant me peace among my enemies and take up my cause for justice now and forever. Amen.

## HAZAEL BECOMES KING

**Scripture**: "... [Hazael] left Elisha, and went to his master Ben-hadad, who said to him, 'What did Elisha say to you?' And he answered, 'He told me that you would certainly recover.' But the next day he took the bedcover and dipped it in water and spread it over the king's face, until he died. And Hazael succeeded him." (2 Kgs 8:14–15)

**Read**: 2 Kings 8:7–15

## From Contemplation to Action

**Reflection**: Ben-hadad II (880–842 BCE), king of Damascus, Aram, is ill, and Hazael, his servant, informs him that Elisha, the man of God, is coming to Damascus. No reason is given for the Israelite prophet going to Gentile territory. Ben-hadad instructs Hazael to take a gift, find Elisha, and divine whether or not he will recover from his sickness. Hazael takes forty camel loads of goods as a gift for the man of God, but the narrative never indicates that he gives them to Elisha or that the prophet accepts them. When Hazael finds Elisha, he declares that he has come from King Ben-hadad, who wants to know if he will recover from his illness.

Playing the role of the biblical trickster, Elisha tells Hazael to tell him that he will recover, but Elisha declares that the LORD has informed him that he will die. This causes Hazael to look intently at Elisha until he becomes conscious that he is staring at him and is ashamed. Meanwhile, Hazael notices that Elisha is weeping. After asking the prophet why he is crying, Elisha, ever the clairvoyant, informs him that the LORD has informed him that Hazael will become king of Aram, and he knows all the evil Hazael will inflict on the people of Israel. He will burn their fortresses, kill their young men with the sword, dash the children's heads on rocks, and rip open pregnant women. After Elisha finishes speaking, Hazael declares that he is insulted. He is no dog, that is, despicable human being, that he would ever do such things. Also, he is no dog of low social status able to accomplish such things. But, again, clairvoyant Elisha states that the LORD has shown him what kind of king he will be over Aram.

At that, Hazael leaves Elisha to return to Ben-hadad, who asks him what Elisha told him. Hazael repeats Elisha's words that Ben-hadad will recover. However, the next day Hazael lives up to the reputation Elisha had already created for him. He takes the wet bed cover and smothers Ben-hadad with it. Then, Hazael (842–806 BCE) becomes king. He becomes king to punish Israel in fulfillment of Elijah's unaccomplished mission (1 Kgs 19:15). He injures King Jehoram (Joram) of Israel (2 Kgs 8:28–29; 9:15). Later in the Second Book of Kings, the narrator writes about the LORD beginning to trim off parts of Israel using the hand of Hazael (2 Kgs 10:32–33; 13:3, 7, 22). Hazael also intended to attack Jerusalem, but King Jehoash of Judah capitulated to him and bribed him with gold (2 Kgs 12:17–18).

While the primary purpose of this account is to conclude the first of Elijah's commissions from the LORD (1 Kgs 19:15) through Elisha, his successor, it also presents the LORD's grand plan to use Hazael as his instrument to punish his people. It must be stated immediately that God punishing people is very distasteful to modern folks, but it was not that way with biblical humans. In the Hebrew Bible (Old Testament), the LORD often punishes evil and unfaithfulness either directly himself or indirectly through his people's enemies, as is the case of Hazael. Thus, biblical writers interpret their people's suffering and defeat in battle as punishment by the LORD. However, people today do not attribute suffering and defeat as God's punishment for unfaithfulness.

The question about how a good God can permit evil to exist is referred to as theodicy. The biblical presentation above about God using Hazael to punish his people is but one of many different theodicies. For example, there is a dualistic theodicy which pictures the world as an arena where the equal forces of good and evil battle to see who will win. St. Augustine explained theodicy as humans with all-powerful-God-given free will who make mistakes and bring evil into the world. In redemptive/atonement theodicy people embrace suffering as part of God's plan for salvation. Evil and suffering occur so people can develop their souls in irenian/evolutionary theodicy. A faith solution states that there is no adequate explanation for evil. God works by persuasion, according to process theodicy; he suffers with people, but he does not punish evil. And in liberation theodicy, suffering is caused by the oppression of others. All of those and many more theodicies permeate the unconsciousness of most people today just like the one that supported the biblical author's perspective thousands of years ago.

**Journal/Meditation**: Do you think God punishes evil? How? If not, what is your primary theodicy? What do you think about the role of Elisha as biblical trickster? Is that an acceptable role to play today?

**Prayer**: All-powerful LORD, you have everything in the world under your control, all good and all evil. To your chosen prophet Elisha, you revealed your plan using Hazael to punish your people. Send your Spirit to me to enlighten me in your ways now and forever and ever. Amen.

## JEHU BECOMES KING

**Scripture**: "Then the prophet Elisha called a member of the company of prophets and said to him, '... [T]ake this flask of oil in your hand, and go to Ramoth-gilead. When you arrive, look there for Jehu.... Then take the flask of oil, pour it on his head, and say, "Thus says the LORD: I anoint you king over Israel."'" (2 Kgs 9:1–3a)

**Read**: 2 Kings 9:1–13

# From Contemplation to Action

**Reflection**: The second of Elijah's commissions (1 Kgs 19:16) is fulfilled at the word of Elisha. He sends a member of the company of prophets to Ramoth-gilead—a town east of the Jordan River in territory disputed by Israel and Aram—with a flask of olive oil in hand to find Jehu, an army commander, anoint him king over Israel, and begin the revolt that will overthrow the last descendant of the house of Omri (Ahab, Ahaziah, and Jehoram [Joram]). When he finds Jehu—son of Jehoshaphat, son of Nimshi—he takes him into an inner chamber, pours the flask of oil on his head, and declares him the new king of Israel at the LORD's word. In the same way, Samuel privately anoints Saul as the first king of Israel (1 Sam 9:27–10:1) and later anoints David the next king of Israel (1 Sam 16:13) in the presence of only his father and seven brothers.

Then, in order to fulfill all that Elisha had predicted, the prophet declares that the LORD, the God of Israel, decrees that Jehu will destroy the Omrides and avenge the blood of the prophets shed by Jezebel, Ahab's queen. Elijah had declared that Ahab's line would come to an end and dogs would drink Jezebel's blood (1 Kgs 21:21–23). Not only are those words repeated by the prophet in the Second Book of Kings, but the same formula recalling the past times when the LORD ended a royal line is also employed. The prophet Ahijah declares that the house of Jeroboam (930–910 BCE) will end (1 Kgs 14:10–11). The prophet Jehu, son of Hanani, declares that the house of Baasha (909–886 BCE) will end (1 Kgs 16:3–4). Jeroboam, Baasha, and Ahab were kings of Israel.

After the member of the company of prophets leaves the commander—now anointed king—Jehu goes to his soldiers, who ask him why the madman came to him in secret. The mention of a prophet as a madman refers to the ecstatic experience often employed by one (Jer 29:26; Hos 9:7). After attempting to pacify them with a non-answer, the soldiers call Jehu a liar. This provokes him to tell them exactly what the unnamed prophet had said: "Thus says the Lord, I anoint you king over Israel" (2 Kgs 9:12b). After Jehu pronounces those words, the soldiers take their cloaks and spread them for Jehu on the steps, indicating their submission to him. Then, they blow a trumpet and proclaim, "Jehu is king" (2 Kgs 9:13).

Jehu wastes no time fulfilling his destiny. He conspires against Jehoram (Joram), King of Israel, killing him with an arrow (2 Kgs 9:24) outside Jezreel. He also shoots King Ahazia of Judah, who is visiting King Jehoram (Joram) of Israel, and he, too, dies (2 Kgs 9:27b). Next, Jehu enters Jezreel, where Jezebel is living, and instructs some of her eunuchs to throw her out a window (2 Kgs 9:33). Jehu writes letters to the guardians of the seventy sons of King Ahab and tells them to bring the heads of the sons to him (2 Kgs 10:7), and when they do so, he kills anyone else associated with the house of Ahab (2 Kgs 10:11, 17), including relatives of King Ahaziah of Israel, who succeeds King Jehoram (Joram) to the throne (2 Kgs 10:13–14). Jehu does this to fulfill the word of the LORD spoken through Elijah (2 Kgs 10:10). He also slays all the worshipers of Baal in Israel (2 Kgs 10:18–29) and demolishes his temple. And the LORD was pleased with what Jehu did (2 Kgs 10:30).

While it may be difficult to see and even harder to accept, the righteousness of God plays itself out according to the historian writing the Second Book of Kings. Right triumphs over wrong. Truth triumphs over false. Life triumphs over death. In other words, the historian perceives a divine plan at work. The plan began with the LORD's instruction on Mount Horeb (Sinai) to Elijah to anoint Jehu king of Israel. Elijah did not complete that mission before he ascended into heaven in a whirlwind. Elisha did complete that mission by sending a member of the company of prophets to anoint Jehu as king of Israel. Immediately, he begins cleansing the house of Ahab of every man, woman, child, and servant. He scours the land of Baal worship and Baal's worshipers. The LORD, the God of Israel, is pleased with Jehu's enthusiasm.

The concept of divine plan underlies much of biblical literature because people presumed that their all-powerful LORD had everything under control. While this may have made them mere pawns in a chess game, it gave them some sense of security that everything had a reason and God was putting in motion another step of his plan. Such enthusiasm for a divine plan is not as prevalent as it once was. Modern people do not think of themselves as puppets manipulated by a powerful LORD. However, while that extreme understanding of a divine plan no longer permeates the consciousness of all but a few, there is some truth still in the preconception. That truth is known through discernment which begins with careful contemplation and reaches an understanding concerning what action should be taken. Thus, while God does not send army commanders to wipe out every living relative and associate of a royal dynasty today—even though that is the way the biblical historian presents it—the LORD does send the Spirit to work quietly within people to instill in them a desire to cooperate with God. Through contemplation, as demonstrated repeatedly by Elisha, one knows what needs to be done, goes, does it, and unfolds the next step of the divine plan.

**Journal/Meditation**: After contemplating the major events of your life, what do think God's plan has been for you? Did you recognize it earlier or later in your life? What difference does cooperating with God make for you? What security do you get from believing that God has a plan for you?

**Prayer**: At your word, O LORD, your prophets anointed new kings and destroyed old dynasties in order to bring your people back to you. Guide me with your Spirit that, knowing what you desire of me, I may strive to further your divine plan now and forever. Amen.

# ARROWS

**Scripture**: Elisha told King Joash of Israel, "'Take the arrows'; and he took them. He said to the king of Israel, 'Strike the ground with them'; he struck three times, and stopped." (2 Kgs 13:18)

**Read**: 2 Kings 13:14–19

**Reflection**: Elisha has grown old and has fallen sick. He is nearing the end of his life. King Jehoash (Joash) of Israel (801–786 BCE) has succeeded King Jehoahaz (816–801 BCE), who has succeeded King Jehu (843–816 BCE); he goes to see Elisha before the prophet dies. When he sees him on his death bed, he shows him respect and declares, "The chariots of Israel and its horsemen" (2 Kgs 13:14b). Jehoash's (Joash) words to Elisha are meant to echo previous episodes of such mystical sight (2 Kgs 2:12a; 6:17b); the words function much the same way as a brand logo does today—they identify Elisha as a man of God. Within a few verses, the chariots of Israel and its horsemen will carry him to God through death, just not with the flare of Elijah's ascent in a whirlwind to heaven in a fiery chariot with fiery horses (2 Kgs 2:11).

Elisha directs the king to perform two symbolic acts which divine Jehoash's (Joash) future. First, Elisha instructs Jehoash (Joash) to take a bow and an arrow and to draw the bow while the man of God places his hand over the king's hand; this gesture will share Elisha's power with the king. Then, Elisha instructs him to open the east window and to shoot the arrow he has drawn in the bow. Once the king has done so, Elisha informs him that he has shot the LORD's arrow of victory at Aram. In other words, King Jehoash (Joash) will lead Israel's army against the Arameans at Aphek, which is east, and defeat the Arameans who have been harassing Israel.

The second symbolic act follows the first one. Elisha tells the king to take the arrows and strike the ground with them. The king, using the divine number, strikes three times and stops. Elisha becomes angry with the king, informing him that the number of times he struck the ground with the arrows is the number of times he will defeat Aram. If he would have struck the ground with the arrows five or six times, he could have destroyed that country. In other words, striking the ground with arrows indicates that Jehoash (Joash) and his army will strike the Arameans with Israelite arrows but not destroy their enemies completely. Indeed, the Second Book of Kings makes clear that King Jehoash (Joash) defeated King Ben-hadad III, son of Hazael, three times, and recovered the towns of Israel (2 Kgs 13:25b).

As his last great wonder while he is still alive, clairvoyant Elisha reveals Jehoash's (Joash) future to him through symbolic or ritual acts that the prophet interprets for the king. Everyone wants to know the future! Fortune tellers read lines on people's hands and, supposedly, tell them their future. Many people would not think of not reading their horoscope in the daily paper or online in order to determine their future. Add in tarot cards and Ouija boards and it is not difficult to conclude that future-telling is a money-making industry. The advantage that the Elisha cycle of stories has over future-tellers today is that the biblical historian only kept the stories about the future that the man of God got right! The accounts that he got wrong were blown away by the winds of Israel to be lost forever. No one can know for sure what the future will bring. Yes, many people, using modern technology coupled with critical-thinking skills, can calculate some of the future, but no one can be as accurate as Elisha is portrayed by the biblical historian.

**Journal/Meditation**: What brand logo(s) do you associate with yourself? Specifically, how do you divine your future? How accurate are you?

**Prayer**: Your mystical chariots and horsemen, O LORD, herald your undeniable presence and disclose your prophet's future. Grant that one day I may be carried by such fiery transportation to the kingdom where you live and reign forever and ever.

## ELISHA'S DEATH

**Scripture**: "As a man was being buried, a marauding band was seen and the man was thrown into the grave of Elisha; as soon as the man touched the bones of Elisha, he came to life and stood on his feet." (2 Kgs 13:21)

## From Contemplation to Action

**Read**: 2 Kings 13:20-21

**Reflection**: In the biblical world, bodies were often placed in caves, which contained shelves carved into the walls. After being wrapped in strips of cloth, the body of the dead was carried into the cave and laid to rest on one of the shelves. Then, a round stone—large enough to cover the entrance to the cave—was rolled into place. After a few years, the cave could be opened and the bones could be collected, put in an ossuary (bone box), and placed below a shelf, which could be used again. All the short account of Elisha's death states is that the man of God died and was buried in such a cave-like tomb. However, death is not the end of Elisha's journey; once born into this world, one never dies.

Some years after Elisha's death during a Moabite invasion of Israel, a man was being buried in the cave-tomb. Those carrying the body saw the marauders and, in order not to draw attention to themselves, quickly threw the body into the cave where Elisha's bones were buried. As soon as the dead man's body touched Elisha's bones, he came back to life and stood on his feet. This miraculous account is recorded to demonstrate that Elisha's power continued even after death in a tomb. His very bones were a conduit for the LORD's life-giving power. In this regard, the prophet's bones are like Elijah's mantle. Both are objects of divine power.

This story may have given rise to the Catholic practice of reverencing the bones of the saints. Referred to as relics, whole bones or parts of bones are often displayed in reliquaries, a precious metal container often containing clear glass so that people can see the bone or bone fragment and venerate the holiness of the person of whose body it once was a part. Relics are often interred under new altars; when a bishop dedicates a new altar, he may place relics under it and seal the opening. The purpose of venerating or contemplating relics and placing them under altars is to present the life of holiness of the saints as examples for contemporary people to imitate or enact.

The author of John's Gospel employs the story about Elisha's bones raising a dead man to life in telling one about Jesus raising Lazarus from the dead as the last of his seven major signs or wonders (John 11:1-44). Lazarus, brother to Mary and Martha, has died and been buried in a cave-like tomb by the time Jesus gets to their home in Bethany. In order to emphasize that Lazarus is really dead, Martha mentions that he has been dead four days (John 11:39); four indicates that he has begun to return to earth. If the stone across the entrance to the tomb is removed, a powerful stench will emerge. Nevertheless, the Johannine Jesus directs that the stone covering the entrance to the tomb be rolled away. Then, after praying, he calls for Lazarus to come out, and the once-dead man walks out with his arms, legs, torso, and feet bound with strips of cloth (John 11:44). There can be little doubt that the Johannine author knew and expanded the tale of Elisha indirectly raising a dead man in order to present the last of seven signs of Jesus' divine status.

Even from the solitude of the grave Elisha works a final wonder that leads to deeper contemplation on the part of those hearing this story. Psalm 94 speaks of Sheol, the first level of ancient people's three-storied universe, as "the land of silence" (Ps 94:17). Likewise, Psalm 115 declares, "The dead do not praise the LORD, nor do any that go down into silence" (Ps 115:17). Ancient people buried their dead in caves because the cave was a portal to the underworld, Sheol, the place where the dead live! Elisha remains unexplainably alive in the underworld and, through the cave-portal, is able to awaken a dead man to life. Lazarus remains unexplainable alive in Sheol, and, through the cave-portal, Jesus summons him back from the underworld to life on the middle level of the three-storied universe.

Contemporary people know that the universe is not created in three stories! Contemporary people know that once a person dies he or she tends to stay dead! No one walking through a cemetery and seeing a coffin-size hole in the ground would conclude that God had raised another person from the dead! Rational thought would dictate that either a dead person was going to be buried in the hole or that one had been exhumed from it. Resurrection of the dead is not available to ordinary experience. Resuscitation may be available through experiences in hospital emergency rooms and surgery centers in which heartbeats are restarted and lungs are inflated with the help of medical machines.

In the world of the eighth century BCE, resurrection was the ability to migrate through the cave-portal from the lower level of the universe, where the dead were sent to live, to the middle level of the universe. The Lukan Jesus builds upon this concept in a unique dialogue with the Sadducees. After stating that "those who are considered worthy of a place in that age and in the resurrection from the dead neither marry nor are given in marriage" (Luke 20:35), he declares that "they cannot die anymore, because they are . . . children of God, being children of the resurrection" (Luke 20:36). Then, to prove his point the Lukan Jesus appeals to the account of Moses and the burning bush in the Hebrew Bible (Old Testament) book of Exodus (3:6):

"... [T]he fact that the dead are raised Moses himself showed, in the story about the bush, where he speaks of the Lord as the God of Abraham, the God of Isaac, and the God of Jacob. Now he is God not of the dead, but of the living; for to him all of them are alive" (Luke 20:37–38). The underworld, Sheol, is the place where the dead live!

With the Copernican revolution and the demise of the conception of the world as built of three stories, the mythology of the cave-portal and, thus, the context for understanding the biblical text disappeared. Today, modern people use heartbeats, brainwaves, and breathing ability to determine whether or not one has passed beyond this life to whatever exists on the other side of death. While metaphors are employed from this side of life to attempt to describe what is on the other side of death, the fact of the matter is that they remain metaphors. The daily pattern of falling asleep at night and waking in the morning provides a good metaphor for death; death is like falling asleep and waking to new life on the other side of death. Likewise, being born into life on this world can be used to describe being born into eternal life on the other side of death. Most people envision resurrection as resuscitation: a dead body is brought back to life. By definition, resurrection cannot be resuscitation! Recognizing that metaphors reveal nothing on the other side of death leaves modern people in the same place it left ancient people: No one knows what is beyond the experience of death.

**Journal/Meditation**: What metaphor do you use the most to talk about what is on the other side of death? What does your metaphor reveal to you? What does your metaphor hide from you? What affect has converting from a biblical three-story universe to a Copernican solar-centered one with infinite space had on biblical literature? How does the Catholic practice of revering bones of the saints, even placing them beneath altars, illustrate resurrection?

**Prayer**: LORD, God of Abraham, God of Isaac, and God of Jacob, you are not God of the dead but of the living. Because I am a child of the resurrection, grant that I may be found worthy of a place in the new age and pass through death to where I will be alive with you forever and ever. Amen.

## ELISHA SUMMARY

**Scripture**: "When Elijah was enveloped in the whirlwind, Elisha was filled with his spirit. He performed twice as many signs, and marvels with every utterance of his mouth." (Sir 48:12ab)

## Elisha

**Read:** Sirach 48:12–14

**Reflection:** The author of Sirach (Ecclesiasticus), Jesus son of Sirach, in the Old Testament (Apocrypha) begins his short reflection on the prophet Elisha in his six-chapter section titled "Hymn in Honor of Our Ancestors" by noting that he was filled with the spirit of Elijah, who was taken to heaven in a whirlwind at the end of his ministry. Because Elisha was filled with Elijah's spirit, Sirach declares that Elisha performed twice as many signs as did Elijah. Elijah feeds the widow of Zarephath and her son, restores the life of the same widow's son, calls upon the LORD's fire to consume his offering on Mount Carmel, makes it rain to end a drought, calls upon the LORD's fire to consume a captain with fifty men two times, and crosses the Jordan River on dry ground by parting the water. While others may include more wonders on Elijah's list, the bare minimum seems to be six. Elisha parts the water of the Jordan River and crosses on dry ground, purifies a spring near Jericho, sends bears after taunting boys, provides oil as revenue for a widow of man belonging to the company of prophets, revives the Shunammite's son, purifies a pot of stew, feeds one hundred men with twenty barley loaves, makes an iron ax head float in the river, heals Naaman's leprosy, and raises a dead man with his bones. While others may include more wonders on Elisha's list, the bare minimum seems to be ten. Thus, Elisha did not perform twice as many signs as Elijah, but he came close to doing so.

Elisha is depicted by the Second Book of Kings's historian as a clairvoyant. This is acknowledged by Sirach; with his words Elisha often predicts the future to rulers. He predicts pools of water in a dry wadi, and water appears; he predicts that the king of Israel will defeat Moab, and he does; he predicts that the Shunammite couple will conceive and bear a son, and they do; he knows where the king of Aram and his army will camp, and that is where the king of Israel finds them; he predicts plenty of food during a siege, and plenty of food is found in the camp of the enemy; he predicts that a captain will not live to enjoy the food, and the captain is trampled to death before he can get to it; he predicts that King Ben-hadad will die, and he dies; and he predicts that King Jehoash (Joash) will defeat the Arameans three times, and he does.

Elisha lives during the reigns of four kings of Israel: Jehoram (Joram) (852–843), Jehu (843–816), Jehoahaz (816–801), and Jehoash (Joash) (801–786). Sirach states that the prophet never trembled before rulers. In many of the tales surrounding him, Elisha serves as the rulers' foil. While loving Israel, he often critiques her kings, their behavior, and the religious tradition they present to their people.

For what Elisha should be best remembered, however, is completing two of the three parts of Elijah's mission which he left undone. It is Elisha who informs Hazael that he will succeed Ben-hadad II as king of Damascus. It is Elisha who sends a member of the company of prophets to anoint Jehu king of Israel. Thus, with those two missions accomplished, the divine plan set in place at the time of Elijah is finished during the time of Elisha.

The last thing Sirach mentions about Elisha is his ability to raise the dead even though the prophet himself had been dead a long time. This leads the author to praise Elisha's many wonders and to declare that even in death his deeds were marvelous. This last deed—raising a dead man with his bones—surpasses Elijah's works for sure.

Elisha embodies the basic premise of this book. Contemplation leads to activity, and activity leads back to contemplation. Yes, Elisha is great in the LORD, who sends Elijah on the mission to find Elisha and anoint him as his successor. Through solitary contemplation followed by activity, Elisha is able to cooperate with his God and further his plan for the Northern Kingdom of Israel. As a conduit for divine power, he is a powerhouse before kings, often trumping their decisions and confounding their plans. He knows the divine plan because he spends time contemplating the work of the LORD. Once he knows the plan, all that remains is to carry it out.

**Journal/Meditation**: What is your favorite wonder done by Elisha? What do you discover by contemplating it? What do you think your role is in the unending unfolding of the divine plan? What activity flows from your contemplation to further the divine plan?

**Prayer**: After enveloping Elijah in a whirlwind, O LORD, you filled Elisha with his spirit, working signs through him and filling his mouth with your word. Send your Spirit to me that I may do your will now and forever and ever. Amen.

# Recent Books by Mark G. Boyer

*Nature Spirituality: Praying with Wind, Water, Earth, Fire*

*A Spirituality of Ageing*

*Caroling through Advent and Christmas: Daily Reflections with Familiar Hymns*

*Weekday Saints: Reflections on Their Scriptures*

*Human Wholeness: A Spirituality of Relationship*

*The Liturgical Environment: What the Documents Say* (third edition)

*A Simple Systematic Mariology*

*Praying Your Way through Luke's Gospel and the Acts of the Apostles*

*Daybreaks: Daily Reflections for Advent and Christmas*

*Daybreaks: Daily Reflections for Lent and Easter*

*An Abecedarian of Animal Spirit Guides: Spiritual Growth through Reflections on Creatures*

*Overcome with Paschal Joy: Chanting through Lent and Easter—Daily Reflections with Familiar Hymns*

*Taking Leave of Your Home: Moving in the Peace of Christ*

*A Spirituality of Mission: Reflections for Holy Week and Easter*

*An Abecedarian of Sacred Trees: Spiritual Growth through Reflections on Woody Plants*

*Divine Presence: Elements of Biblical Theophanies*

*Fruit of the Vine: A Biblical Spirituality of Wine*

## Recent Books by Mark G. Boyer

*Names for Jesus: Reflections for Advent and Christmas*

*Talk to God and Listen to the Casual Reply: Experiencing the Spirituality of John Denver*

*Christ Our Passover Has Been Sacrificed: A Guide through Paschal Mystery Spirituality—Mystical Theology in* The Roman Missal

*Rosary Primer: The Prayers, The Mysteries, and the New Testament*

www.ingramcontent.com/pod-product-compliance
Lightning Source LLC
Chambersburg PA
CBHW070930160426
43193CB00011B/1640